A LIFE AMID CRISIS

A MEMOIR BY LORD
ZION

"If all we have is right now, what happens
when you don't know what to do with it?"

Published by His Lordship's Endeavours

A CIP Catalogue record for this book is available from the British Library.

The moral rights of the author have been asserted.

Cover photo by Neil Henderson. Additional photography by Gary Burchell

Design by ebook-designs.co.uk

Printed by CreateSpace

ISBN: 978-1535047364

www.lordzion.com

DEDICATIONS:

For Vikki who has taught me more and helped me more than she will ever know. Remarkable, considering her diminutive size.

Mum. Among my fondest memories are those of us cooking sausages on a camping stove during the strikes of the 70s. Thank you for that. And thank you for introducing me to the enlightening world of foul language.

Dad. A million thank-yous for everything you have done for me wouldn't even come close to covering it all. My greatest wish would be for you to be able to adopt me.

Gary. Best. Brother. Ever. Sorry for abandoning you on the cross Channel ferry in a toilet full of potential nonces. It was nothing personal. Thank you for bringing Louise, Jake and Kara into my life.

Granddad Burchell for treating me no differently.

My family at large to whom I owe various degrees of thanks.

Ditto friends.

DEADICATIONS:

My Baxter Grandparents whose hard work, integrity and generosity humble me daily. I only wish they were around to see some of the good stuff I did. I like to think it would have made them proud. On occasions.

Nanny Burchell who was always so kind and loving. It would be amazing to hear her exclaim "oooooh!" just one last time.

Vikki's Granddad Pete and Nanny Dulcie who I came to love as if they were mine.

CONTENTS

INTRODUCTION:
THE BIT BEFORE
THE BOOK

Most of you don't know me but, that's OK because I don't know me either. I used to. I used to know myself very well. I was one of those cocky bastards who pretty much decided out of the gate what he wanted to do when he "grew up" and did what was necessary to get there. In a fashion.

However, the last few years have put all that in turmoil. I never believed in the notion of a mid-life crisis, feeling it was something that people of a certain age made up as an excuse to have one last fling with outrage before getting on that conveyor belt to the grave. No way was that going to happen to me! But I think it did. Or has. Or is. Not quite worked it out yet.

Whether we like it or not, age and ageing changes our outlook on life; gives certain things a different perspective. Also, with age comes increased knowledge. If you have half a brain-cell, you will apply that new found knowledge to aspects of your journey to make it easier and better. Or, as in my case, just more confusing.

Learning is something that I enjoy. Having had some rather hilarious brain issues, I have spent many years absorbing what info I can about the mind, human behaviour and why it is we do those things that we do. Some of it seems logical, other bits completely bonkers and the left overs... well, we just sweep them under the carpet, for now. When I apply this to myself, it helps me try and understand some of my behaviours and, to a large extent, that is what this book is about: an exploration into why I turned out the way I did and how all that is now conspiring against my new-found existence.

Hey, we all have problems, right? I am not unique in that respect. But I am unique. In the same way that you are, your neighbour is and everyone that we meet. It appears to me that most people are stuck in a rut and drift through life without asking the very important questions. Am I happy? What could I do to improve my situation? Am I where I want to be in life? Am I doing what I want to be doing? For me, that last one is key and the reason I am writing this.

It wasn't all that long ago I had it all sussed. I was in a fairly successful rock band, doing cool things like making albums, videos, touring, playing festivals.. Y'know, all that good stuff. Then I started getting a little nagging voice that kept asking me, "are you REALLY enjoying this?" and, eventually, I had to answer it, "no".

Bugger. So, now what? Having devoted half my life toward this quest, this goal, this vocation, can I really just turn my back on it? Well, yes, I can. Should I? That is a whole other question. I have lost my purpose in life, and I need to find it again.

In writing this book, I am hoping to come to some conclusions. I have many interests in life and ideas on how I can turn those interests into exciting career opportunities. I am discovering enlightenment for the first time, and I wasn't even looking for it. I need to work this shit out. I need to ask the right questions. I need to prevent becoming a fucking hippy.

 MOST PEOPLE ARE STUCK IN A RUT AND DRIFT THROUGH LIFE WITHOUT ASKING THE VERY IMPORTANT QUESTIONS. AM I HAPPY? WHAT COULD I DO TO IMPROVE MY SITUATION? AM I WHERE I WANT TO BE IN LIFE? AM I DOING WHAT I WANT TO BE DOING?"

CHAPTER 1:
THE £50,000 CHEQUE

I am holding in my hands a cheque for £50,000. This is my cheque. Made out to me. Has my name on it and everything. I even take a photo of it on my smartphone, evidence for my future self that I did at least once have a little bit of money.

Up until this moment, this cheque had been a concept. I knew it was coming. Earlier in the year, my nan had died after a long battle with Alzheimer's. My granddad had died some ten years prior and I was aware they had been wealthy. How wealthy, I didn't know, but we were really close and it was my understanding that I would be left something.

Of course, it is an awkward question to bring up, asking your mother as you help clear her mother's house several months later, "So, is there anything for us grandchildren?".

"No." was the reply. "I don't think so." She confers with dad who confirms to the negative. "Oh." is just about all I can muster as hurt and confusion hit me, along with one of those horribly warm sensations as your blood scoots around trying to determine which bit of you is in trouble.

I speak with Vikki – my partner of 13 years – on the way home about this. "It isn't about the money, it is about what it represents." is the only way I could try and describe what I was feeling.

I've never been all about the money, see. If I was, I reckon I'd be pretty rich by now. I'm fairly clever and driven so, if I was willing to do a whole bunch of stuff I didn't want to do just for the cash, I am certain I would have a lot of it. But my motivations have always been driven by my morbidity; a fear of death that has resulted in me spending most of my life trying to gain a small bit of immortality in the form of fame. More specifically, as a rock star.

It didn't quite work out the way my 15 year old self saw it working, but I did alright. More on that later; back to the journey home.

"My grandparents were really loving people, but not overly huggy and I don't remember them ever saying 'I love you'. The way I understood that they loved me, the way they taught me love, was to give me food and money. Not excessive amounts (of money, food-wise, I was fed to bursting point) but occasional bounties that made me feel special."

Vikki didn't dive out of the car in disgust at what could be construed as greed, so I carried on.

"This was their last chance to say 'I love you' and they didn't take it."

I really was hurt. I had to explain this to mum. After all, these were her parents and I didn't want her to think this was all about the money.

"I just don't think it is common for grandparents to leave their grandchildren anything." was the best reasoning she could come up with.

I wasn't buying it. I was glad, in a way, to find that my brother felt the same way: hurt and confused. All for the same reasons, too. Perhaps we misunderstood our relationship with them? Maybe we

I'VE NEVER BEEN ALL ABOUT THE MONEY, SEE. IF I WAS, I RECKON I'D BE PRETTY RICH BY NOW. I'M FAIRLY CLEVER AND DRIVEN SO, IF I WAS WILLING TO DO A WHOLE BUNCH OF STUFF I DIDN'T WANT TO DO JUST FOR THE CASH, I AM CERTAIN I WOULD HAVE A LOT OF IT."

weren't quite as special as we thought we were? Have we been looking at them with rose-tinted glasses?

Then mum rang. She had looked at the Final Will & Testament and bit more thoroughly. "I think you might be included. Just a nominal amount though, £500".

To this day, I have no idea where that figure came from. It was nice to hear though, even if the amount did seem surprisingly small. In some ways, more surprising than not being included at all.

Another call.

"I have re-read it and I think that you get 12.5% of the cash."

Bingo! Now, that is more like it. Suddenly, I *did* know my grandparents well. REALLY well, in fact. I had surmised that, knowing granddad, he would have given his two daughters 25% and his four grandchildren 12.5%. That was pure Granddad Logic and I was fucking right. Phew, they did love me after all!

My brother and I forgave our mum. After all, she was grieving and had a lot of things to deal with and face. We were just glad it was sorted out and we could move on without having to go into any kind of therapy. Naturally, though, we couldn't help speculate on the amount. We have never been privy to any accounts and, although it was clear that granddad had built a successful business, they were never, ever flashy with money. (Although they did buy a flat in Littlehampton, just so we had somewhere to go and have a cup of tea..).

So, I had to ask. "It should be at least £10,000," mum said, "maybe a bit more". Cool! £10k. Ten grand. Ten G's. I could do something quite useful with that.

To this day, I have no idea where that figure came from. And, as I sit in Lloyds trying to open my first bank account in a decade, I stare at this cheque – with the promise of almost £30,000 more to come – and wonder who this makes me.

Somehow, this has changed my self-identity and I needed to add this inheritance onto the ever growing list of confusions and complications that had so upturned my life in the past few years.

But I'm not complaining, honest!

CHAPTER II:
ALLOW ME TO INTRODUCE MYSELF

My name is Zion. Hello! Zion is my full name, having dropped my surname some 24 years ago in a fit of familial confusion. Plus, as a wannabe rock star, my first name seemed to have a certain amount of gravitas, so it was a completely logical decision to make.

It has caused me no end of grief ever since. This is a typical conversation with any institution I encounter:

"Name?"

"Zion."

"Is that your first name or surname?"

"It's the whole thing. I only have one name."

"What do you mean, you only have one name?"

"Well, it is like having two names, but only half as much."

They never like that bit.

"You can't have just one name."

"Well, you tell that to the Passport Office and Driving License Agency as there is only one name on both of those documents."

"Wait there, I will have to speak with my manager".

It. Never. Ends.

I bought myself a Lordship in my late 20s. I was fed up with people calling me "Mr Zion", as Zion was my first name, it felt weird. A Lordship would fix that.

They now call me "Mr Lord Zion". Such is life.

I wasted an awful lot of time as a wannabe rock star in my 20s. I blame Nirvana. It was all going swimmingly until "Smells Like Teen Spirit" burst my bubble. The band I was in was getting decent gigs, we had management, even the offer of a record deal. This shit was EASY. I was going to be a Glam Metal Superstar on a huge ego trip around the world...

Those jangly three chords changed everything. I went from being a Sexy Rock God to Out Of Touch Loser practically overnight. I just couldn't understand why anyone would want to look like that and listen to music like that. It would appear I was in a minority.

Being pre-internet days, if you didn't have the press on your side, you were doomed. Kerrang! Magazine was no longer printing the little bits I was sending in and all my efforts to convince myself it was just a phase was simply a lie in disguise. I knew what was going on, I could see it. I just couldn't admit it. Hell, even I hated most of what rock had become: a bloated facsimile of itself and had lost it's edge. If I had been a bit older when Nirvana struck, I am sure I would have been just as caught up in it's plaid wave as everyone else.

But I stuck with my cowboy boots.

And I struggled. Oh, how I struggled. A valiant fight was put up, trying to remind people how much fun rock could be. My band, 'King Bitch, won a Battle of the Bands and some recording time, but that didn't help. Then my guitar player-slash-writing partner left to work in Monaco so I just sodded around for a bit. Like, a few years, a bit.

I BOUGHT MYSELF A LORDSHIP IN MY LATE 20S. I WAS FED UP WITH PEOPLE CALLING ME "MR ZION", AS ZION WAS MY FIRST NAME, IT FELT WEIRD. A LORDSHIP WOULD FIX THAT."

Life moves on at such a slow pace to be almost imperceptible. But those seconds that mount to minutes soon fill an hour that turns into days which convert nicely to months right before they launch into years. Enough of that and you get a bloody decade. Shit, where did *that* time go?

At 28, I found myself alone, lonely and hideously in debt. To sustain my awesome rock star life-in-absentia, I was dealing in vintage Star Wars memorabilia. Soon, so was everyone else so I switched to importing the fledgling DVD format. For a brief moment in time, I was raking it in. The internet had been invented by now and I had an early internet shop. Dammit, I was a fucking pioneer! Exploring this Brave New World of eCommerce, excited by the opportunities, able to see the potential, not quite as able to see the sodding thieving bastards who managed to nick £7k off me.

I tried to stave off the inevitable, borrowing from the same loving grandparents that feature in Chapter One, but the downward slope had started. The bank was being next to fucking useless and any money that came in just served bank charges.

It was around this time that a shock of pink hair entered my life in the curvy shape of Vikki. A lustful fancy turned into a deep friendship that morphed into love and, before we knew it, our lives were intertwined and my problems were shared. Being 18, Vikki didn't have any problems. Being a generous kind of guy, I let her have mine.

We drank. A lot. We had sex. A lot. We enjoyed each other and had a lot of fun. A lot. There was a recklessness to our passion but it was only going to end one of two ways. Lucky for me, Vikki isn't an easy pushover and we could see that we were going nowhere fast so needed to straighten ourselves out, or end up homeless and destitute.

Somehow, we found the wherewithal to do this. All the time still drinking and having sex. A lot. Gotta have priorities, right? She already knew how to play bass and we liked being around each other, so why not start a band? And that's what we did: some-when in 2002, SPiT LiKE THiS emerged from our glistening genitals into the world.

Having learnt the lesson of my recent past and deciding that being poor was not much use when you had rock n' roll world domination to plan, we also started an online business, SMELLYOURMUM.COM. By this stage, I had accumulated a raft of slogan ideas for T-shirts so I designed them, Vikki learnt to screen print and, before we knew it, people were giving us money to sell them offensive words on garments of wearable cotton. By happy, well designed coincidence, these were the self same people that would probably buy our music.

And it only bloody well worked! Our guerilla marketing techniques spread the word about the T-Shirts and the music world wide. We honed, we gigged, we toured, we recorded, we mucked about, we got mucky, we worked hard, we worked smart. In 2010 we reached, what I now look back on and understand to be, the peak. We put a brilliant line-up together, had killer tunes, recorded our second album with a legendary producer, played a festival in Ibiza, headlined another on Guernsey then drove all the way to Germany to play on the same bill as Iron Fucking Maiden at the Wacken Festival.

EVERYTHING we had worked so hard for had paid off. We were an internationally recognised band and, although we weren't earning bucket loads of cash, we were further up the bumpy road to doing so than 99.9% of bands that ever form.

Nothing, absolutely nothing, was going to stop us now.

CHAPTER III:
THE DODGY KNEE

There were several things that were signposting that this was the End Of The Beginning (glass half full, Zion, glass half full), but nothing more so than my dodgy knee.

It was 2012 when I fulfilled a lifetime's ambition to visit the Italian ruins of Pompeii. I was completely spellbound by the whole experience and never wanted it to end. We had a full itinerary though and Mount Vesuvius to climb. Unbelievably, it was closed because of the rain (maybe they thought we might slip and fall in) leaving us with time to kill, so we looked for something to do.

We found Herculaneum. Not "found" as in "discovered" - someone else had done that many decades before – but "found" as in "oh, here it is". Covered in the same 79AD quake juice that destroyed Pompeii, Herculaneum was much better preserved. Whereas Pompeii feels like a frozen moment in time, Herculaneum is more like a building site. So-much-so I am pretty certain that, if I visited now, it would be finished.

It was spectacular. Not as good as Pompeii, but still something to see. Vikki and I were veracious explorers of these lonely ruins: up and down stairs, in and out of buildings, not quite believing how much had been recovered. I must have taken a million photographs.

And here – I believe – is where the flaw in my plan to remain forever young was exposed for the sham it truly was. The problem with taking a million photographs is that the batteries in the camera need constant changing. I would take myself into an elegant Roman ante chamber, get down on my haunches to find the batteries deep in my rucksack and swap them over. So what, right? Ordinarily, yes, but I was wearing extremely tight trousers. So what, RIGHT? Well, ordinarily, yes, but these were trousers of the spray on variety that did an awesomely fantastic job of showing off my shapely legs. They also did an equally marvellous job of shutting off any blood to my lower limbs and causing seemingly permanent damage to the sciatic nerve that runs down my left leg.

Oh.

I didn't know, at the time, that this was the problem. I became aware that something wasn't playing ball when an excruciating pain circled my knee making it virtually impossible to walk. I didn't feel a snap, twang or break, just a very isolated pain so severe that it rendered me pretty fucking useless.

Now, ladies and gentlemen of the jury, I know what you are thinking: that I am a chap and, therefore, a bit of a big girl's blouse when it comes to illness, injury or pain. Well, you would be wrong. I am not like that at all. Having grown up in a household that rushed you to the doctor's at the slightest sniffle, I have aged into a hardy fellow that is nary knocked down by much at all. So for me to be hobbling along, pathetically, was quite out of character.

Of course, I thought this pain would be temporary and, within an hour or so – maybe an overnight rest – it would right itself and I could continue my gallivant. Next morning, however, the pain was still there. The plane ride didn't shake it and nor did a proper good sleep in my very

NOW, LADIES AND GENTLEMEN OF THE JURY, I KNOW WHAT YOU ARE THINKING: THAT I AM A CHAP AND, THEREFORE, A BIT OF A BIG GIRL'S BLOUSE WHEN IT COMES TO ILLNESS, INJURY OR PAIN. WELL, YOU WOULD BE WRONG."

own bed. The agony continued for a week, then a month, then several bloody months. In fact, it was nearly six months before I could go up and down stairs without having to support myself with the banister.

Naturally, I took myself to the doctors. After the six months of pain. By then, there was fuck all they could do. It wasn't the knee (as I thought it was seeing as all the pain was centred around it), but most likely nerve damage. Nerve damage that could take years to heal 100%. As I write, it is over four years since this damage occurred, and, although considerably better, it does still cause me problems.

As someone who exercises very regularly, I found this minor disability extremely hard to cope with. I had to find new ways to exercise and even new ways to walk. Driving a manual car was made especially difficult and, worst of all, my energetic live concert performances were also greatly affected.

Beyond the physical limitations, there was a mental hurdle I had to get over. I have always felt fit, indestructible and, due to my physical activities, have remained quite young looking. My features bely my true age and keeping trim continued to fool people into thinking me a good 10 years younger than I actually was. The fact that the injury occurred slightly less than six months before turning 40 probably did not help.

Was age really creeping up on me like an uninvited and unwelcome visitor? Bollocks, fuck, tits and arse, I do believe it was.

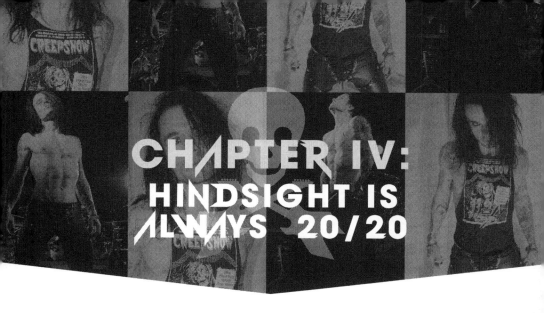

CHAPTER IV:
HINDSIGHT IS
ALWAYS 20/20

2010. What an incredibly exciting time for SPiT LiKE THiS. After years of live performances, a slight balls up with our debut album, months of writing and rehearsing, we were as ready as we could possibly be to record album number two. I already knew the title – Normalityville Horror – and the producer was chosen the year before.

Chris Tsangarides. To those in the know, that is a name that will send shivers down your spine. Starting his illustrious career on Thin Lizzy, graduating with Gary Moore, becoming legendary with Ozzy Osbourne, a damn near Grammy winner with Judas Priest and a movie star with Anvil. In short, having that man behind the desk guaranteed one thing: we were going to make an amazing album.

And we did. I am as proud today of that album as I was the second we finished recording it. Beyond the pre-production stage, the actual recording was hard work: 19 days in total. I was there for every second, conducting my band through every note and beat whilst CT recorded each track to the best of his sonic abilities. It is a fantastic sounding album.

A lot of the time recording was spent idly chatting with CT about my hopes and dreams, about how I felt we had been screwed over by various people, about how we still held lofty ambitions. He listened intently, sympathised where appropriate and encouraged when necessary.

Little did I know that he was also plotting something that would become clear a few months later.

Before all this, we were in Ibiza giving our new guitar player his debut in front of a very hot and sweaty crowd. Great gig, great times. Being paid to travel to foreign climes to play rock n' roll... it IS the dream.

No time to dwell on that though, we had the Channel Island of Guernsey to get to as we were headlining the Saturday night of the Chaos biker festival. Guernsey has always felt like home from home for me, having travelled there umpteen times as a child. Indeed, it was also the place I chose to fly to when I finally conquered my fear of flying just a few months earlier.

Blazing 80 degree days, every day meant that Vikki and I explored virtually every inch of that island on our bicycles, camping under the stars each night. We had six days there and just one performance to do. It was free holiday time – a well deserved free holiday – and we squeezed every ounce of enjoyment out of it that we could.

Within a few days of finishing the album, it was time for the final big trip of the year. Our then (German) manager, Ralph, had managed to get us a slot on the prestigious Wacken festival, one of the biggest music festivals in the world. We were elated, ecstatic and eager, sharing the bill with heroes such as Mötley Crüe, Alice Cooper, Slayer and Iron Maiden. A boat trip, a damn long drive, a camp site conundrum and we (eventually) made it.

The highest of all high hopes hinged on our time there. Ralph had arranged for some German labels to see us and he was fairly

WE WERE ELATED, ECSTATIC AND EAGER, SHARING THE BILL WITH HEROES SUCH AS MÖTLEY CRÜE, ALICE COOPER, SLAYER AND IRON MAIDEN. A BOAT TRIP, A DAMN LONG DRIVE, A CAMP SITE CONUNDRUM AND WE (EVENTUALLY) MADE IT."

convinced - and convincing - that a record deal would be easy pickings. We were up against Alice Cooper, but it didn't worry me too much. After all, there were about 80,000 people there and they can't ALL want to see Alice?

Well, yes, actually, they can. Disappointingly, we played to a much smaller than anticipated audience, our stage complete with a boxing ring in front of it. I remember bouncing on it, surprised at quite how springy it was. Regardless, we were there to do the job of kicking some ass and we did do just that.

Breathlessly, we awaited Ralph's verdict. Did we get signed? Well, no, not yet, but an A&R guy did like us and an arrangement was made for us to play in the press tent. I didn't really know what this entailed but, hell, another gig at Wacken – awesome!

Early next morning, we found ourselves in the press tent. No stage, as such, and seating for the press to whom standing is anathema. Never mind, we would give it our all. We did. We sweated for 20 wet minutes and finished with a climax that Ron Jeremy would be proud of.

Certain that we had done enough, we dried ourselves off, went out into the midday sun and enjoyed interview after interview, photo after photo, signing after signing. Clearly, rock superstardom was – literally – just around the corner.

Exhausted and elated, we started our long journey home. After a week sweating in a tent in the middle of a dusty field, I enjoyed (for the first time ever) a shower in the stop-off hotel. I didn't grumble once on the 12 hour drive and the slow ferry across the channel felt like a speedboat to destiny.

I could not wait to get back and start fielding the many offers we no doubt will have received.

CHAPTER V:
BOLLY POG

B olly was a dog. Correction, a pog. I never liked dogs, you see, but when I met Vikki she came with one so I had to adapt. My way of justifying this hypocritical behaviour was to reassign Bolly's designated mammalian term into one that I could accept. Hence, she forever became a pog.

The dislike of dogs started at a very early age. We didn't have anything other than rabbits or fish at home, so I wasn't really exposed to them often. When I was, they seemed unnecessarily shouty and I could see, clearly, some sharp teeth. I also didn't find them particularly nice to look at. When, one day, a dog leapt over the fences to attack one of mum's rabbits, their fate was sealed: I hated dogs.

It's one of the things I became known for. I would spew typical teenage garbage about how we should "learn to love each other before loving an animal" and other angst ridden Goth nonsense. Of course, there is an element of truth to that, but I have since learned that love is not a finite commodity.

I was quite happy Not Liking Dogs. It didn't affect me; I didn't need to like them. Even when I lived in a house whose population exploded by some 200+ assorted animals, not one of them was canine.

Then I met Vikki. She had a dog, her constant companion since the age of 14. An animal that helped her through troubled teenage times as well as offer some protection from the mean streets of London. If hot knicker action was to remain on the menu, I was going to have to somehow come to terms with the existence of this creature.

As it happens, it was very easy. An initial slight wariness and distrust of each other soon grew into a very fond friendship. Over the 11 years that Bolly became my dog too, I fell in love with that hairy, ginger beast. Vikki was always the leader of her pack, but I did end up second in command and I know that Bolly would have laid down her life to protect me.

Gladly, it never came to that. Healthy right up until her last day, Bolly lived to the ripe old age of 16. The saddest decision of our lives together gave Vikki and I the chance to ease her on her journey as we stroked and hugged her to rest.

I was devastated. I needed to be strong for Vikki – she would be suffering more – and we did support each other through the grieving process and beyond. Bolly is now a wonderfully fond memory and it is only upon recounting her passing that I feel anything other than joy when she bounds into my brain.

It was a few years later that I dreamed of having another dog. Not in a wistful way, but in a pictures-in-your-head-whilst-fast-asleep way. By strange coincidence, just a few days later Vikki brought up the subject of getting a dog. A small dog. A very different dog to Bolly, but a dog, none-the-less.

I was cautiously agreeable. I still wasn't a *dog fan* and the only pog in existence had departed this earth. I had to lay down some ground rules, number one being that I could look at it and think it "cute" rather than the apathy I feel when I look at most dogs.

I'm a cat person, see. Nearly all cats are beautiful, mysterious creatures with a "fuck you" attitude I admire. They are the supermodels of the animal kingdom and I fully expect to turn into a mad old cat lady one day. Fortunately, I have managed to limit this to one white, deaf cat who has become my personal creepy stalker and a little wobbly dwarf cat with neurological problems that means she falls over a lot. Hilarious. I do love my little disabled buddies.

So, cuteness was a factor. After all, I was going to have to look at this thing every day and, if I was to stand a chance of liking it, this was the head start I needed.

However, I did not count on getting so bored looking at the pictures of dogs Vikki showed me. One dog in need of rescue blurred into another. All worthy causes in need of a new home and, after a little while, I had had enough.

"Yeah, that one." I don't think I even looked up.

We went and collected Skully in September 2013. At the rescue place, we waited to see if the dog we had come to see would be friendly or not. Then this teeny tiny puppy came bounding out, the rear half of her a blur of excited happiness. She immediately leapt up at both me and Vikki, clearly understanding that we were the people she needed to impress.

Sold!

And she is a cutie. Part Jack Russell, part Chihuahua. She has the markings and temperament of a Jack, combined with the size, ears and heat-seeking need of a Chihuahua. She is adorable and so friendly. She's not quite the guard dog Bolly was (we are her guard people), but she plays nicely – kind of – with the cats and has sticky-out Yoda ears, so what more could we ask for...?

The lesson learned is that we *can* change and adapt long-held beliefs. It isn't healthy or wise to cling on to the same ideas and ideals as your teenage self. Some of them may still hold true, but an awful lot of them are just knee jerk reactions to an affectation cultivated to make you interesting or to stand out. That is OK, all kids do it as a way of trying to find out who they are. However, when it seeps into adulthood and limits your potential pleasures or informs your decision making, it is time to have a re-think.

Losing Bolly was a life changer. Getting Skully was a game changer. If only she came with a volume knob.

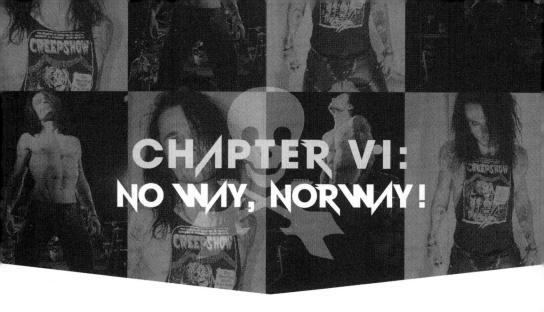

CHAPTER VI:
NO WAY, NORWAY!

Did I mention the best thing about being in a band is the overseas travel? Of course, that is somewhat tempered by the fact that you tend to only view these exotic locations through a plane, train or automobile window, but you do at least get a feel for a country.

Norway was one such place. We first visited in 2011 to play Sandnes and Oslo. When our agent rang to say that we had shows, my immediate response was "great, let us know when and I can get the plane tickets sorted".

"No, no, that is all paid for.", replied Martin.

"Oh, cool! Well, let us know the locations so I can get Vikki looking for hotels."

"No need, they are covered too."

"Blimey! You'll be telling us we get paid next!"

"You are."

And that is how our very first completely all-expenses paid mini-tour of a foreign country came about. We had been overseas before, but there was always one of those ingredients missing. Either we had to pay for the travel or accommodation (or both) out of our gig fees, or we got travel and lodgings but no fee. You would be amazed how rare the magic combo of All Bases Covered is.

The trip to Norway was an amazing adventure. It was everything we could want it to be. Collected from the airport by our host, Jon, driven to Sandnes, we were treated like rock ambassadors. There was even a massive article about us in the local newspaper (not that we could read it, mind). And the hotel? Four star all the way, baby!

Oslo was slightly different. Less of a four star hotel and more of a hostel above a brothel. No bother, we were rock n' rollers so shrug off such things. Just give us a crowd, give us a venue and we will win them over.

Except, in Oslo, we didn't. Looking back, this was the first tiny little inkling that something had changed. The first chink in the armour. The support band were really good. From Sweden, they had the songs, look, youth and attitude that appeals across the board. Suddenly, we weren't the most interesting act on stage. Nor the youngest. Nor the best that night.

This shook me to my core. I tried to shrug it off. After all, we couldn't bring our assortment of usual stage props; we couldn't speak the language; we were tired; the smoke machine was drying out my throat. The excuses piled up. The fact of the matter was, with the introduction of an older guitar player, our demographic had shifted from being a band that skewed toward youth to one that – literally in my case - hobbled toward middle age. In one brush stroke, we'd lost the young female market – the one we often relied upon to make the most noise and get excited around us. That bloody support band had 'em though.

Never mind. It was a great adventure and, although it got to me at the time, I presumed it a temporary glitch and got over it. If we now appealed to a more mature crowd, we would just have to win them over. No problem. Promises were made to return to Norway - I wanted it to be a bi-annual pilgrimage.

I didn't know it at the time, but my next all-expenses-paid visit to Norway would have nothing to do with music. At all.

CHΛPTER VII:
THE 70S

The 1970s was a very important decade in Great Britain. For me, in particular, as I was born two years into it. I don't recall my initial impressions but, as the years have gone on and I can look back, I see how it shaped Zion v1.0.

I was a little racist. It was the prevailing wind of the times, I'm afraid. Television had programmes like "Love Thy Neighbour" and "Mind Your Language", so casual racism was part of the fabric of the country. There was also the National Front: a hard right faction, similar to the BNP, but more forthright in their hatred of any non-whites. They had a snazzy eye catching logo, not too dissimilar to the Nazi swastika, which was easy to draw on school books.

Of course, those of us that did (and there were a lot) didn't understand what we were doing, or what it stood for and I am glad to say that most of us grew up to be fine members of society who, if anything, are more racially tolerant, probably due to some inherent guilt at our childhood behaviours.

I don't recall the exact moment I decided not to be racist any more, but I do remember often wondering why we were supposed to dislike people that were a different shade to us. By my understanding, we were all pretty much the same inside and, the very few coloured children at school seemed OK to me. I mean, I played with some and came away unscathed. I actually secretly liked a couple.

But I was dealing with my own problems to care too much about the problems of others. I was relentlessly tormented and bullied on a daily basis throughout the three years of first school. It lessened slightly when I reached middle school and stayed at a constant trickle through most of secondary school. In fact, it was only really when I reached 16 and did a life changing performance (more on that later) that the bullying stopped and a strange, distant, disconcerting respect replaced it.

As a child, I was chubby. I was also very pretty, often mistaken for a girl (unbelievably, still am) and had a stupid name. "Zion, wee-on, the big fat pee-on" was the playground chant that I heard several times a day, every day. Is it any wonder that I still have weight concerns nearly 40 years later? These things stick like superglue.

There was the typical violence: dead arms, dead legs, Chinese burns (racist), punches to the stomach. Thankfully, they left the face alone. More than the physical pain, it was the anguished "why?" that hurt the most. Before going to school, I had no pre-conceived notions of it. I believed I was just like all the other kids around. It didn't take me long to understand that, for some reason beyond my control, I was different. Something put me on people's radar, even though I was a timid church mouse. I had the X-factor before it was a thing. Sadly, when you are five, that tends to mean that some alpha brat will bully you and try to make you cry.

A bit like the modern day X-Factor, in fact.

It didn't help much that I was also trying to process the not insignificant fact that my sperm father had walked out on my mum and they were getting a divorce. This was not a common thing back then and, for a long time, I was the only person I knew whose parents had split. Hard to believe now!

He was a ladies man and didn't want to be held down by a wife and child. He was also a drummer and had the dreams that go along with that. I couldn't understand this at the time, all I knew was that my dad had left and I didn't know what this ultimately meant. How could I? I had no-one to ask and mum was dealing with her own pain.

We made a good team, me and mum. Kept each other company. I have fond memories of cooking meals in the lounge on a little gas stove as there were constant power cuts back then. Sounds far from idyllic, but they are among my most treasured memories. Something about the smell of bacon and eggs, frying away over a little gas burner, sitting in the near dark with my mum felt so comforting. I'm glad we had that.

Mum eventually met the man who was to become My Dad; look after me, love me, protect me and also give me a baby brother. From that respect, I won the lottery. Unfortunately, dad number one kept cropping up, affecting my mental stability as I tried to cope with confused feelings and his idle (non physical) threats.

For many years I let this weigh me down. Those events became a fear of abandonment that lead to some pretty abominable behaviour once I reached my teens and started getting girlfriends. Jealousy was very much an issue and I needed to control my environment and the people within it. This lead to violence, something of which I am deeply ashamed. I know I made people unhappy and scared to be around me, and I wish that wasn't the case.

Not until my late 20s did I realise that you cannot truly control people and all the fears about abandonment or jealousy just turn into one self-fulfilling prophecy after another. If you want someone to leave you, just keep telling them that one day they will. Every single time they will assure you that they won't leave, until they do.

Jealousy is not something that I harbour any more. I don't covet others' possessions and I no longer see those in my life as possessions for me to do with as I see fit. I have learned to nurture, support and encourage rather than belittle, condemn and ridicule. I don't fear abandonment because everyone will leave you one day, even if it is by death, but life will continue and it will sort itself out, eventually.

As for that little racist? Well, the final light bulb moment was when I got into bodybuilding. My favourite bodybuilder (Shawn Ray, for those that give a shit) was a black American guy. I thought he looked amazing and he inspired my early workouts. Genetically, he was by far my superior and, in interviews, he came across as a nice, intelligent bloke. What the hell had I been thinking? Indoctrinated into an idea that was not fact-based, borne out of fear and ignorance, I dropped that last veil of racism.

Fear and ignorance has a lot to answer for. It leads to bullying. It leads to self-limitations. It leads to living a life blinkered, struggling to maintain the status quo as anything else seems scarily impossible. Even if what you are trying to maintain makes you unhappy. Learning is the only way out of this trap. But you have to be willing. You have to want to escape.

FEAR AND IGNORANCE HAS A LOT TO ANSWER FOR. IT LEADS TO BULLYING. IT LEADS TO SELF-LIMITATIONS. IT LEADS TO LIVING A LIFE BLINKERED, STRUGGLING TO MAINTAIN THE STATUS QUO AS ANYTHING ELSE SEEMS SCARILY IMPOSSIBLE."

CHAPTER VIII:
THE LAST GREAT TOUR

A s a band, we had enjoyed many great gigs, support slots, festivals and tours. In May 2011, we embarked on a tour that I presumed was a mere springboard to the amazing tours to come. Several dates up and down the UK with glam metal legends, Tigertailz.

Tiger-what-now? Tigertailz. Back in the day (80s/early 90s), Tigertailz were the UKs answer to Mötley Crüe. Huge glam rock hair, big riffs, bigger choruses. I loved 'em so much, the album cover to their biggest album, "Berzerk", was the image on my 18th Birthday cake. The 18 year old me worshipped them so, to now be on the road with them was both exciting and fun.

To be honest, it wasn't the first time we had played with bands that I grew up idolising. Most notable was LA Guns. They were probably my favourite band during the glam metal era. Dirty sounding songs that made you feel bad ass just by listening to them. Sadly, "don't meet your idols" is a truism. Enough. Back to the 'Tailz!

The opening night gig was in Birmingham. It had been a shitty drive up and the venue was one of those right awkward bastards to get in and out of. We also had to contend with the egos of the road crew of a band that were performing in the much larger, attached venue, who were making our lives just that bit more tricky than they needed to be. Egos of road crew. Fucking unbelievable.

We were rushed and we felt it. It didn't help that some idiot left the house lights up until about half way through our set. It's weird when that happens. Both audience and band have a sense of feeling very awkward but neither are sure why. It is only when the faux pas is noticed and the lights dim that you realise what the problem was. Oddly, it can be helpful not to see too much of an audience (and they can be a right ugly bunch...kidding!), and the audience would much rather be watching a band spotlit, swathed in colour, than in the kind of lighting you might get in your front room.

Aside from this opening gig, the rest of the tour was great. Two shows in particular remain steadfast in my mind as being Fucking Awesome. One was in London at the Underworld, a venue we had played many times before. The other was the Cathouse in Glasgow. Our first time there and it was a giant sweaty bollock monster of a show.

Although we were the support act, we were well known and, therefore, often reviewed alongside the headliners. I am proud to say that we were compared favourably and, in many cases, the reviewer's choice for the night. Kill your idols.

If only we could do this week after week, month after month. I still hated the driving (final day of the tour I had to drive from Glasgow to Nottingham, unload, do a show, pack up then drive from Nottingham to home which, back then, was way down south) but loved the performance and the adulation. We all felt like that: on top of the world. We were performing songs we had yet to release and they were going down a storm.

Imagine how much better it will be once the next album is out. Imagine how much bigger we will be. Imagine the kinds of tours we can go on...

CHAPTER IX:
HOW DID I GET HERE?

I'm not talking the birds and the bees – I am going to guess you know all about that sticky mess – but how did I end up on stage? After all, I was a shy child and was never a gregarious sort. I have always been a bit of a show off, though, albeit a reluctant one.

My first performance in front of an audience was an out-and-out very elaborate lie. It was attention seeking at its very finest and was also the first clue that I may have one or two loose screws. The fact that my parents never thought to stop me has often baffled me; maybe I lied to them as to the real reason I needed a Cossack outfit, urgently.

I was eight, had recently moved into middle school and clearly wanted to stand out. When asked if anyone had any hobbies, my hand shot up. Unfortunately, this happened – along with my mouth speaking – before my brain engaged with any kind of common sense.

"Cossack dancing", was my answer. Immediately, I had the interest of the entire class and, I suspect, a very dubious teacher. "Oh really? Tell me more."

"I do it in London, a couple of times a week." London seemed glamorous. All the major events that I lied about happened in London. I got shot in the leg with a rubber bullet by the IRA in London. I learned to read and write Japanese in London. And, of course, my Cossack dancing lessons happened in London. I was one of the few kids that had actually been to London but, from what I recall, Cossacks were thin on the ground. At least they were in the early 80s.

"You must do a demonstration", said the teacher, "Of course!", said I.

Clearly, I was an idiot. An idiot without a plan. Or any Cossack dancing tuition. I did, however, have a costume that mum had made me for a fancy dress event (that I pulled out of last minute - I always did that) and thought it could be adapted. What emotional blackmail I laid on mum to get her to re-tailor this outfit, I don't recall. A week later, I was ready.

In America, they call this "Show and Tell". The child stands at the front of the class, demonstrates their skill and explains the machinations of it. I was to do the same.

By this stage, I had – in the way of all truly great liars and sociopaths – convinced myself that the falsehood was true. This was real Walter Mitty stuff. I had my soundtrack ("Kalinka") and then attempted the Cossack Dance for the second time in my life. This involved me crouching down on my haunches and kind of bouncing; kicking an alternate leg in the air with each bob.

I impressed the hell out of myself. I then fielded a raft of questions before sitting back in my seat, in full Cossack garb, to bathe in the rather misguided glory that I was certain this strange pretend hobby of mine would bring.

Things calmed down for me on the Cossack dancing front over the years that followed. I had my small audiences whom I would impress with my Japanese writing but, on the whole, I remained the kid at the back of the school nativity dressed as a shepherd.

This continued until I was 16. I had always enjoyed drama at school; loved creating, directing, learning, rehearsing then performing little skits within the confines of a 45 minute lesson. The drama teacher encouraged me somewhat and, who knows, if they had remained my drama teacher, perhaps my life would have taken a different course.

But they didn't. I enrolled in GCSE drama but got transferred to a class run by a right miserable bastard of a teacher who had his favourites: the loud mouthed kids that were in his class already (one particularly brash loud mouth is a copper now...go figure). Every lesson, it was these monstrosities of misplaced ego that were thrust into the spot light to bore us shitless with their crappy postulations and vague attempts at acting.

Clearly, I wasn't bitter. Slowly I slunk to the back of the class, realising that my only role in this was as a scene painter or other behind-the-scenes job. Still, I did enjoy the buzz on those days when performances happened and I rallied around, doing my bit for all concerned. Like a fucking hero.

However, one day, something caught my ear. "The school are putting on a new event called the Pop Mime", said the teacher, who is dead now. I sat upright in my chair to listen fervently, "So we are looking for some of you to put together something to demonstrate to the school what this competition is about." For the second time in my life, my arm shot up involuntarily. I must get that looked at.

I think I surprised Mr Benson (yes, that was the bastard's name) with my enthusiasm. But I was one of very few volunteers so he had little choice in selecting me. Now, I don't entirely recall how events transpired over the next few weeks, but my "band" was put together made up of my best pals; our roles chosen (I was the singer) and the band/song choice done: Def Leppard's "Pour Some Sugar On Me".

Our school was pretty big, about 1,500 pupils I believe. It was divided into two campuses, each with a large hall and impressive stage. There were to be two performances, one in each building, both during morning assembly.

Nervously, I hit the stage on day one to pretend-sing (or mime, as it indeed was) my heart out to the backing track. I was Joe Elliott, albeit a slightly ruder one as, on the lyric "shake it up", I found myself gesticulating the "wanker" sign toward all the gathered teachers. The kids enjoyed this no end and it was the final lesson I needed in my "How To Shock To Get Positive Attention From Impressionable People" class (of which I was the only – and star - pupil). Up until that point, I had mostly learned by studying Frankie Goes To Hollywood.

The final barres of the song came. I held my arms aloft like I had seen so many rock stars do and held my breath... A mighty roar filled the hall and I felt a feeling I had never felt before. I needed to bottle that shit and take it daily. Alternatively, I could become a Rock Star.

From that moment, this was the goal. The following year, another Pop Mime. By now, Guns N Roses had surpassed Def Leppard in my affections and their bad assness was rubbing off. On the evening of the show (the final – teachers, pupils and parents were in), I was prepared with my trump card.

I can see it in slow motion. The look of horror on the face of my form teacher, Mr Greatorex, as I pulled it out. The encouraging nods from my fellow band mates as I shook it about. The wide eyed disbelief of the pupils in the audience as I jettisoned forth the head froth and sticky liquid (of a can of beer I had smuggled in, filthy).

Clearly, I was now a Fucking Legend and much respect was thrown my way by all - except the teachers and parents. I discovered this the next day when summoned to the Head Teacher's office. To my surprise, I was not there to be congratulated and fast tracked to the role of Most Awesome Pupil Ever, but to be informed that there had "been complaints" and, therefore, I was now and forever banned from doing the Pop Mime.

Well, fuck you, because I'm going to do this shit for real.

 A MIGHTY ROAR FILLED THE HALL AND I FELT A FEELING I HAD NEVER FELT BEFORE. I NEEDED TO BOTTLE THAT SHIT AND TAKE IT DAILY. ALTERNATIVELY, I COULD BECOME A ROCK STAR."

CHAPTER X:
MEANWHILE, IN GERMANY

I t was not good news. Our manager, Ralph, had done what he could to secure us a record deal but, despite a great reputation as a band, hard work and a solid product, things just did not work out.

There was a silver lining though. Chris Tsangarides had been in touch: he was putting together a record label and he wanted to sign us to it! We were elated. Having CT as our label boss would be perfect. He is well known, well respected, has industry contacts and is a thoroughly nice bloke. We met up and he explained his plans for the label. They sounded exciting and matched our own lofty ambitions.

We were IN. He mentioned a business partner a few times and, eventually, we were invited to meet him. Vikki and I drove to Dover for the meeting with CT and Dave Cousins, founding member of Prog Rock luminaries, The Strawbs. I was very familiar with The Strawbs as they were one of my dad's favourite bands. In fact, one of the few rebellious tales he tells is of the time he did a moonie from the stage at a Strawbs concert to get a free LP (a fine example of how the deteriorating inherent value of music has affected the consumer – you wouldn't get anyone do a moonie for a free MP3, they'd just nick the fucker).

Dave was a really nice bloke, too. And, again, a total legend in the business; well respected and knowledgable. Between them there was

70+ years experience: it could not fail. It was such a positive meeting, too. I told them the plans I had for SLT, as well as letting them know all the neat little tricks I had learned as an online retailer of eight years standing. This combined knowledge, along with determination and hard work, could really see the label – and SLT – going places.

Of course, no deal is ever set in stone until the ink dries on the paper. Honestly, I thought it would be wrapped up in a few weeks (this was late 2010) but negotiations, re-negotiations, procrastinations and life events meant that the signing did not take place until early in 2012. Originally, we were going to sign it with both Dave and CT present but, for reasons I now forget, CT couldn't make it and it was going to be postponed (for the second time). I pushed back though and the date was agreed, with or without CT. Vikki and I drove to Dave's house in Deal and signed on the dotted line. It was a great day and a blessed relief.

Finally, the world to whom I had been bragging, was going to get to hear "Normalityville Horror". Almost immediately the wheels were set in motion and I was instructed to get all the artwork complete. That was no bother as the artwork had been commissioned 18 months earlier and was just about finished. Still, it was a hard slog to meet the deadlines, but meet them I did.

The plans as had been discussed, never quite materialised. That's OK though, plans in the music business – in all business – need to be elastic and flexible. If something is too rigid it breaks, so I wasn't overly concerned. As long as there was a rough idea, it should be OK.

Just a rough idea, that's all.

CHAPTER XI:
THE UNQUIET MIND

F or as long as I can remember, I have had a busy brain. A thought process that seems almost independent of the input I generate; keen to show me who's boss.

I didn't realise there was a problem when I was young. I grew up hearing voices and, not knowing any different or any better, thought that was what everyone's head was like. An internal monologue, perhaps? No, this was something quite different. It would get loud, domineering and appear as if over my shoulder. It was almost a cloud of noise. It wasn't until I hit my late teens that it became a big problem. As a troubled eight year old, I went to my first psychiatrist. A family psychiatrist. Mum came along with me and we discussed who-knows-what together. I didn't have behavioural issues but have always been somewhat morbid and maudlin (understatement of the fucking century). Over the years, this has become an almost paralysing fear of death, which is a cruel irony in a person who also suffered suicidal impulses, as these two sides battled for supremacy.

We all have problems. I understand that. I also believe that everyone will get "depressed" at one stage in their lifetime. The difference between those people and a person with clinical depression is that the latter is not triggered by a traumatic event; it is a physical thing gone wrong. It is part of the DNA.

For me, it is a lack of serotonin. This means that the little sparks that send messages around my brain don't work very well. This creates short cuts to unhappiness; leaving my head all wired up wrong. Most clinical depression is this, which is why most drugs prescribed are designed to increase serotonin levels. Those same drugs tend to carry a lot of side affects, however.

My fear of death got really intense in my early 20s. I was going through a particularly hard time mentally and something triggered an episode which lasted several years. Every single waking moment was spent thinking about dying and death. Life seemed futile and pointless. We live to die was just about the only conclusion to anything I could reach.

In some, this is a motivational force. It drives them to create a lasting legacy. In others, it throws them into a deep pit of despair. I landed somewhere inbetween. On the one hand, I did want to achieve immortality via fame but, on the other hand, I was continually paralysed by the world around me.

I could barely watch television. I was like that character on the Fast Show who would paint the wonderful surroundings before turning the world on it's head, declaring everything "black" as he covered his work with it's light-less hue. Virtually everything on TV would remind me of death. The most extreme example I recall was a Kodak advert whose motto was "the colours of life". I could not even tolerate that slogan, they may as well have splashed "ZION IS GOING TO DIE" across the screen.

You can only live so long under those conditions before you drive yourself mad(der). It was when I held a knife up to the throat of a house

I WAS LIKE THAT CHARACTER ON THE FAST SHOW WHO WOULD PAINT THE WONDERFUL SURROUNDINGS BEFORE TURNING THE WORLD ON IT'S HEAD, DECLARING EVERYTHING "BLACK" AS HE COVERED HIS WORK WITH IT'S LIGHT-LESS HUE."

mate that I finally realised things had gotten out of control and saw a psychiatrist.

And so began many years of pharmaceutical trial and error, combined with psychotherapy and cognitive behaviour thought therapy (CBT).

I first thought that I was going to kill myself in my mid 20s. I was alone at my house, my world view was bleak and I could find no reason to stay alive. I scribbled note after note to the loved ones I was about to leave behind, almost automatically writing whatever words were sent through the ether via my body to the pen. They looked like they were written by a mad man. Truth be told, I think they were. Screaming and wailing like a banshee, my plan was to gas myself in my garage. I didn't want to die, but I could not think of a viable alternative.

A sealed garage fills with car fumes fast.

Self preservation kicked in. An instinct greater that the will to die: an urge to live. I called the Samaritans which gave me just enough hope to seek help. I did. I ran out of the house and walked for miles until I found a doctor.

Thankfully, I haven't had an episode like that for a while now. I used to drink heavily, which did not help the situation and, on the whole, my life has improved immeasurably since I stopped abusing my body with alcohol. It didn't cure everything, though.

The bad brain wore on, wearing me out mentally in the process. Vikki – by now in my life – was witness to this. She couldn't understand it and feared for me. The scary thing was, I had lost the fear. No longer did the thought of death terrify me. There was almost a comfort in it. I wouldn't have to worry about it any more. Strange logic. One day, in tears, I confided in her the realisation that my life would probably end prematurely - by my own hands.

Vikki isn't one to sit by and take notes, she takes action and she got me to the doctors quick smart. Further trial and error with drugs commenced until, eventually, I found something that really seemed to work: Zyban. In the UK, it isn't a drug used to battle depression, so it was a bit of a fight to get it but, almost immediately, it started to unravel my brain. My senses heightened and I came out of myself. The world no longer seemed a scary, intimidating place and, for the first time I can remember, I felt like I wanted to be part of it.

L-Theanine has been another wonderstuff for me, helping me to cope better with stress. Between them my life has been enriched. As one wall in front of me collapses, I build one behind me. I am determined that those old foes will not rear their ugly head in mine ever again. I am determined not to go backward.

I have a new appreciation of life and want to fill it with new experiences and joy. I have come to the understanding that happiness starts from within and it is up to me to seek it. Often, easier said than done.

But at least I am trying.

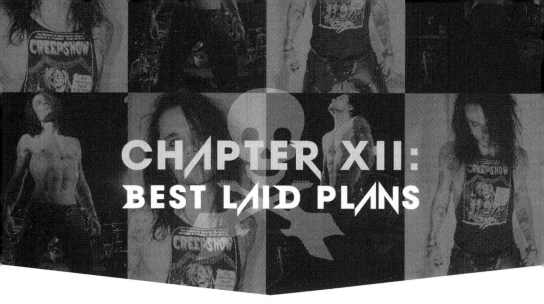

CHAPTER XII:
BEST LAID PLANS

What follows is a list of factual occurrences as I perceive them. I am not writing this account to bitch and moan about events or people; or to complain that things could have been done better. The past cannot be changed – you can only try to learn from it - and whatever path you find yourself on as a result of the past is the only thing you can try and control. Right now is all we have. Yesterday has gone, tomorrow may never come.

That being said, the label did make a right balls up with the release of our album.

To my mind, it is easy. Coordinate and plan between label, band, manager and agent. With all four working together as one, they create a supportive environment that picks up the ball whenever one is dropped.

Dark Lord Records did things different. They wouldn't listen to the band, any scheduling was hopeless as they missed deadline after deadline and all the money they had was put into the wrong places. It drove me a little bit crazy at the time; it was a logic I couldn't understand. My ideas were not taken into account. We were being shown who was boss but it was to everyone's detriment.

Our album eventually came out in May 2012, nearly two years after it was recorded and 18 months since negotiations began. There was no advertising and the press (PR) campaign was run by a couple of girls that were doing things at fanzine level. In short, I could have done it better myself. And did, calling in favours from old press buddies around the world to generate *something*.

The reviews were good, but it didn't help much. No-one pushed to get our video or single playlisted and, without regular airplay, a product dies on its feet.

However, the craziest decision was yet to come. The digital release of the album was held back. In these days where most music is sold via download, the only product available was physical. It didn't take me long to find torrent sites around the world servicing the gaping hole in the digital market.

Apparently, there was a plan. This was to release the digital album in the UK at the same time as both the physical and digital release across Europe. OK. I didn't quite understand the logic but, maybe, they knew what they were doing.

We pushed for information regarding the release. When is it happening? We were losing momentum. One date became another. This was crazy! Were we deliberately being fucked in the arse or was this just old school methods being poorly executed in a new school environment?

Either way, it was a disaster. Without warning, without fanfare, without notification and after months of us asking for a date, the album was released digitally across Europe and the UK one day in April. No-one told us, I literally found out by accident. What the fuck was going on??

It was part of the "plan". When asked what the plan was, there was no answer. Mainly because there was no plan. What followed was more wasted money as a small PR campaign (using an agency suggested by the distributors despite us having a PR guy in place who actively liked us, was a fan and knew exactly where our market was) got underway. We got a smattering of press, for a release that had either already happened, or was coming soon. Did I fail to mention that the physical copy wasn't released across Europe for another SIX MONTHS?

Right at that moment, the final nail was in the coffin lid for Normalityville Horror. All momentum had gone. We couldn't coordinate a tour with interested agents across Europe because we couldn't tell them when anything was going to be released. Initially, it was August. Then September. When I first heard this new date I said, "no later as we are too busy from October to help with the release". It came out in November.

They did the album release equivalent of knocking on someone's letterbox then running away.

At the time I thought – hoped – that we could salvage something. Turns out I was wrong. Not only had they destroyed the album, they may well have destroyed the band.

WE COULDN'T COORDINATE A TOUR WITH INTERESTED AGENTS ACROSS EUROPE BECAUSE WE COULDN'T TELL THEM WHEN ANYTHING WAS GOING TO BE RELEASED. INITIALLY, IT WAS AUGUST. THEN SEPTEMBER. WHEN I FIRST HEARD THIS NEW DATE I SAID, "NO LATER AS WE ARE TOO BUSY FROM OCTOBER TO HELP WITH THE RELEASE". IT CAME OUT IN NOVEMBER."

CHAPTER XIII: GRANDDAD

My Granddad was my hero. He was one of two men who really showed me what being a chap was all about. Not the bullshit, chest beating, club waving man of yesteryear but a solid, dependable human being that people looked up to and respected.

I thought my Granddad was the dog's bollocks. Born 1918 into poverty, he grew up in the East End of London with little in the way of prospects. Tuberculosis nearly killed him before he reached teenage and left him profoundly deaf for the rest of his life. He had no education to speak of but he did have the mind of an engineer.

Like most from that era, he learned to ride a motorcycle whilst very young and, having no money, had to improvise his way through it's maintenance. This gave him good grounding in mechanics and working with his hands.

He first met my nan when she was just 14. Two years his junior, they courted and my granddad would make his way from his dingy surroundings to her more affluent Surrey district. As their romance grew, he used to take my nan out on the motorcycle; she would always encourage him to "go faster, George".

By now, he had taught himself electrical engineering and, with his father, set up a small firm. They would work together with the fledgling Wates housebuilding company, wiring up houses, estates and, eventually, developments. It was a hand-to-mouth existence: they would do the work, collect their money for the day, use that money to buy the supplies they needed to work the next day.

It was a risk, but they had little other choice and nothing to lose.

World War II interrupted things and my granddad was called up. During this time, he and my nan got married. I have a beautiful photograph of their wedding day, the young people I never met. My granddad in his army gear, both of them forced to grow up fast in a world that may not be there for them tomorrow.

Lucky for me though, it was. Granddad was discharged eventually for health issues and borrowed a small amount of money from my nan to re-start his firm. To further make ends meet, after a hard days' work, he would continue into the small hours making wooden toys to sell.

My aunt was born during a bombing raid in 1945; my mum a few years later in 1949. Studying photographs of my mum and aunt from their childhood, it was clear that my grandparents had started to earn a few bob. They purchased the house they would call home in 1955 and lived in it until both of their deaths. It was a lovely house, big but not grand with a large garden that we loved to play in.

Thanks to the war-time bombing raids across south east England, there was plenty of building work going on so my granddad's electrical engineering company boomed. He worked all the hours he could to make sure that his family wanted for nothing. I once asked him what drove him to work so hard and he told me that it was to provide for his children and their respective families. That struck me.

He had his first heart attack before I was born, allegedly shortly after my mum's pregnancy was announced. He was a tough bugger though and barely missed a beat (no pun intended), refusing to take it more easily. I wasn't overly aware of his health issues as I grew up; to me, he seemed indestructible.

I cherish every second I spent with him and my nan. They were always loving and kind to me, took my cousin and I on special trips and spoiled us with sweets and pocket money. I was only about six or seven when I realised that they would one day die. I cried myself to sleep.

The recession of the late 80s forced my Granddad to retire in 1990, aged 70. He didn't want to, but he saw that it was time as his once extremely profitable business was losing money. Fifty years after he started, BCH Electrical Contractors Ltd ceased trading.

Clearly, he had made enough money for him and my nan to continue with life comfortably. They were never showy with their cash, though. The last car Granddad purchased was a Mercedes Benz in 1985. He bought it new, but kept it for the rest of his life.

We would often talk about money and it was always intimated that I would be remembered in their will. I didn't like to talk or think about that stuff much though and I never could get Granddad to divulge to me quite how wealthy they were. The only clues I would get would be when he would bemoan the tax he paid in the 70s, "for every million we turned over, nearly 90% went on tax". Damn!

The phone rang one day. Granddad had had a stroke. After getting off the telephone from my bewildered nan, I broke down in tears. I assumed this was the end. Of course, I was wrong. Granddad was made of much tougher stuff. He was left a changed man, however.

He never fully got his speech back and I learned to lip read, just as I had learned as a child to speak looking directly at him so he could lip read me. He also lost a lot of weight and had to give up his driving license. He never gave up his car though. I guess he kept it in hope that he would one day get to drive it again. He didn't remain without a vehicle, however, and would terrorise Great Bookham charging

 I CHERISH EVERY SECOND I SPENT WITH HIM AND MY NAN. THEY WERE ALWAYS LOVING AND KIND TO ME, TOOK MY COUSIN AND I ON SPECIAL TRIPS AND SPOILED US WITH SWEETS AND POCKET MONEY. I WAS ONLY ABOUT SIX OR SEVEN WHEN I REALISED THAT THEY WOULD ONE DAY DIE. I CRIED MYSELF TO SLEEP."

around on his mobility scooter. He was once stopped by the police for driving to Leatherhead in it. Stubborn man.

I didn't realise the last time I saw him that it would be. Since his stroke, he had been in and out of hospital a bit. I am not even entirely sure why. Maybe he was keeping something from us, or maybe his weakened body was just gradually giving out. His mind never did.

The last contact I had with him was in hospital. I visited regularly and figured he would be home again soon, like he always was. I would sit on the chair next to his bed and he would hold out his hand with his stubby little fingers for me to hold. I don't think I ever told him how much I loved him, but I know he knew.

Then, one day, he was gone. Just like that. No goodbye, just gone. That strong force who had done so much hard work so his family could have a better life, disappeared out of mine. I couldn't face it at the time and, even to this day, I haven't been inside the funeral service of a grandparent. I don't need to see that box; I just write my own tribute and cry a lot.

Granddad has remained with me though. I now occasionally get one of his eyebrow hairs, and I am often thinking "what would Granddad do?" when faced with a tricky dilemma. Since my nan died, I have also acquired a lot of their personal artefacts, along with some furniture that they had had so long it went from fashionable to unfashionable to retro and now, vintage.

Oh, and the not-so-small matter of that £80,000.

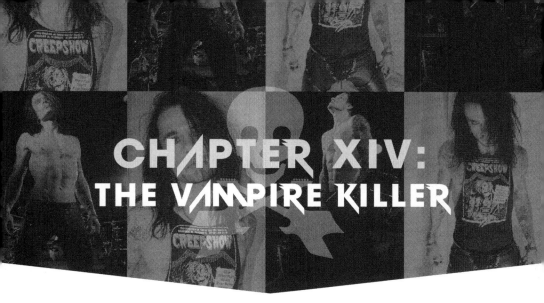

CHAPTER XIV:
THE VAMPIRE KILLER

S hortly after the (delayed) release of our album, we got a
support slot opening for William Control, aka Aiden, at the 02
in London. A pretty big gig and our first for a little while. I was
nursing my bad leg by this point, so had decided to only do big gigs
for the time being.

We were second band on a four band bill in a two band venue, so it
was a tight squeeze backstage and even tighter on stage. Having to
get changed in toilets is never fun; this was made harder by trying to
bandage my knee whilst contorting in awkward positions. The fact that
someone had made a large deposit in the non-flushing toilet didn't
endear me to the place.

Nevertheless, I am a Pro, so got on with it without complaint
and tried to chat to the other bands. They were friendly and young.
Very young. One band had a buzz around them, they were called the
Fearless Vampire Killers. Cool name, I thought, and they seemed to be
putting in a lot of effort to their stage gear. I was keen to talk to them to
find out more. I spoke to the bass player.

"When I was at school, I used to get loads of your stickers and
plaster them all over the place", he said. "I feel really bad that you are
opening for us now."

Ouch.

Whether or not he was being a dick, it was a slap in the face. We had stagnated, whilst these young bands were overtaking us. In short, we'd got fucking lazy.

The gig went alright. I was conscious of my leg, of not being able to give 100%, but the audience seemed to be very positive and got into us. I came offstage feeling pretty good about the whole thing, even knowing that I wasn't in top form.

The Fearless Vampire Killers were up next. I wanted to see what all the fuss was about because, from what I could make out, most of the audience was there to see them. They burst onto the stage in a cloud of talc, added to their clothes to make them appear like dusty old relics. All their clothes were old fashioned, like they were a Victorian rock band. They looked really good. I didn't like the songs much, but I couldn't fault the enthusiasm or the stage craft.

They reminded me of what SLT was like five years hence. And in that moment, I had the words of the Crème Brûlé character from The League Of Gentlemen ringing in my ears: "it's a young man's game"...

CHAPTER XV:
THE BIG 4-OH

T he fact that my leg injury occurred in the year of my 40th Birthday added insult to injury. Literally. I have been blessed with youthful features, a decent hairline and, thanks to my relentless exercise schedule, a ripped body. Most often, people guess about 10 years younger than I am, so I was quite happy to live in denial. My real age was a trade secret; only a very few knew what it really was.

For the first time in my life though, I was feeling my age. Or at least older than normal. I couldn't do what I used to be able to do. I was still hobbling around so any comments about my age or a lacklustre performance would hit me hard.

I banned Birthday cards with "40" on them. I instructed Vikki to let my mum and dad know that, if I went to their house and saw any "40" banners, I would turn straight around again. Partly this was said in jest, but there was a bit of me that was quite horrified at the approaching milestone.

Most people deal with their 40th by having a mid-life crisis of sorts. Thing was, I don't think of it as mid-life. Looking at my contemporaries, many haven't fared well, but me..? I still looked pretty good. I already had the sports car and the younger girlfriend, so how the hell would a mid-life crisis manifest itself in the Land of Zion? A hair cut, sensible car and age-appropriate wife? No, exactly.

So I continued on as I always had. As it happens, I did treat myself to a new car in my 40th year. A dream car: a Porsche 928 S4. It wasn't my first Porsche (fourth), but it was my first 928. I was scared to get it – they have a certain reputation regarding enthusiastic wallet draining – but perhaps it was the looming Birthday that made me eventually say "fuck it".

The car broke down on my 40th. Bummed me out, naturally, and did put a slight dent in my mood. I smiled through it but, inside, I was reeling. It felt like the universe was trying to tell me something. Sad but true. I was having a full-blown pity party, not a Birthday party.

As it happens, once I reached and surpassed 40, I kind of got to like it. This was unexpected. I pretty much denied my entire 30s, quite happy for people to guess me in my 20s (albeit late 20s) but, once I actually made it to 40, I felt suddenly very proud and grown up. Not in a sensible way but in a deserving of respect way. After all, you learn and experience a lot over 40 years, so people do often defer to your better judgement. Bloody right too.

I am now 44. I like 44. I liked 40, 41, 42 and 43 as well. I suspect I will enjoy my 40s until I start nudging toward 50, then I will probably freak out again. But, for now, my 40s are great. I have more confidence than I have ever had and am making very positive changes in my life. OK, some aspects of it do suck. I ache more, get tired easier and am finding it harder to stay devoid of body fat, but I remind myself that it won't get better, so enjoy it for what it is.

The weirdest thing is that I am now at an age that I clearly remember my mum being at. I was in my mid-teens, so the memory of mum in her early 40s is very clear to me. She seemed quite old to

 I AM NOW 44. I LIKE 44. I LIKED 40, 41, 42 AND 43 AS WELL. I SUSPECT I WILL ENJOY MY 40S UNTIL I START NUDGING TOWARD 50, THEN I WILL PROBABLY FREAK OUT AGAIN. BUT, FOR NOW, MY 40S ARE GREAT."

me at the time, especially as she was poorly and had to undergo a major operation. I look at my young nephew, Jake, and figure that he probably looks at me the same way I used to look at people of my age and think them ANCIENT. That's alright, he'll understand himself, one day. Hopefully I will be around to see that.

How much my age affected my outlook on the band, I am not sure. Comfort has always been something I have craved, so I don't think it is that. Although there is something very undignified about getting changed in a room with a shitty toilet, that is undignified at any age. There are also examples – many examples – of people older than me that still rock like fuck, and I know I still can. Maybe I was just aware that there are other things I can do, and I want to do them before it is too late. Maybe I was just being restless. Maybe I was bored.

Frankly, though, I think I had just had enough.

CHAPTER XVI:
IBIZA

Our album was finally released late May, 2012. It was a relief, I can tell you. Until you actually see the album in people's hands, you almost don't believe it will happen. And we really do have amazing fans; they were sending us photos of themselves with their new albums. On top of that, all the reviews that were coming in were positive. Most were above-average-to-very-good which, for a band without a massive PR machine behind it is very encouraging.

So we headed out for our second appearance at the Hard Rock Hell festival in Ibiza feeling cocky, cocksure and excited. Good times were, no doubt, ahead.

We bumped into punk band Vice Squad at the airport. Vikki is a long-time friend of Vice Squad, responsible for pet-sitting when she was a teen living in London. On the flight, guitar player Paul plonked himself next to us and we had a great flight catching up. I was pleased of this; they have long been aware of us and I wanted to show them what we were made of. I wanted them to be proud of what Vikki had become and what she had achieved in her own band.

As with all great plans, things don't always run as smoothly as you hope they might. For a start, our time slot. We went from having a pretty decent slot to – possibly – the worst slot of the whole festival.

AFTER the headline act, very early in the am. Never good. Fortunately, we have enough of a reputation for people to stick around so it was with a warm heart that we took to the stage in front of a decent crowd. Decent, but very, very drunk!

Looking into the crowd, I saw Beki and Paul from Vice Squad. "Let's show them what SLT are all about", I thought to myself.

It wasn't long before things started going tits up. First of all, drum problems. Always fucking drum problems. Our drummer took forever to sort his shit out and, even after all that time, it was never quite right. Today it was worse than ever. Did he just fall off the stool? How about starting sometime soon? Then there was Vikki's bass. Or lead. Or amp. Shit. Something wasn't working. All this time, I am standing on stage like a jilted bride, awkward, all eyes on me. I fucking HATE this shit. We need roadies. We should be above this BS by now.

After the false start, we kicked off. At first it felt good. I wasn't hearing too well through the monitors, which always makes performing harder, but it wasn't the first time. The first couple of songs go straight from one into the other. The idea is that there is a tiny beat-pause before song three, "Zero To Sixty", kicks off. As has happened a hundred times before, the drummer chooses this moment to fiddle with a cymbal, his penis, or something else he didn't sort out initially.

Momentum: gone. Lost. Once it has gone, it is really hard to get back. I have no banter planned, I am expecting to be bopping again by now. The audience starts shifting. They sense that something isn't quite right and it makes them feel awkward. Fact: regardless of how well you play, if you are CONFIDENT and DELIVER, the audience won't notice flaws, they will just get involved and have a good time.

But I was not confident and we did not deliver. Somewhere along

 FACT: REGARDLESS OF HOW WELL YOU PLAY, IF YOU ARE CONFIDENT AND DELIVER, THE AUDIENCE WON'T NOTICE FLAWS, THEY WILL JUST GET INVOLVED AND HAVE A GOOD TIME."

the line, I had lost the faith. Like a priest questioning the existence of God, I was questioning the validity of SLT as a totally kick-ass rock band. Up until recently, there was no doubt. I knew it. I FUCKING KNEW IT. We were a bona fide threat to anyone that shared the stage with us. Not any more though.

To this day, I cannot figure out the moment the last piece of the jigsaw got lost. Did it happen all at once or was it a gradual decline? Was it a self-fulfilling prophecy? Was it because of my injury? After all, I know that I wasn't performing at my best and, with all best intentions, that does affect your head space. It is hard being the front man at the best of times; when you aren't 100%, it is darn near an impossible task.

Back to the gig. The crowd was thinning. We weren't good enough to retain their attention. They'd seen a few songs, dug them, but now fancied going and getting more booze. Harder than that was the look of disappointment on Beki and Paul's faces. Hell, they didn't even stick around 'til the end to pay us lip service and fill the air with false platitudes. Would it have helped? It can do, I wouldn't have believed it though.

Shame. Once upon a time, they would have witnessed Vikki in a mighty fine band. Now I felt we were an unprofessional rabble.

Our agent, Martin, was kind. Full of the usual excuses that a good agent will fill your head with. Bad sound. Bad monitors. Bad time slot. All the stuff to make you feel better about a shitty gig. After all, every band has a shitty gig, it is just that we seemed to be making a habit of it now.

A couple of days later, I bumped into Martin in one of the bars and we got chatting. Had he noticed my leg problem? Yes. He didn't think I was as animated as normal and I was moving kind of funny. Damn. He then said something to me that stuck, really stuck. He said I should go to the doctors to get it looked at and fixed, "after all, that is your living right there".

Fuck. He wasn't wrong.

CHAPTER XVII:
THE LAND SHARK

S omewhere along the way, 2012 did see me achieve an ambition. A dream. Not that I particularly worked hard for it, but a bit of good fortune, a bit of cheek and, let's not kid ourselves, a bunch of cash later, I got a 1989 Porsche 928 S4 – The Land Shark.

OK, I appreciate that a lot of readers won't know what a 928 is. Even fewer probably won't give a shit and might be tempted to skip a chapter about a car, fearful that I will fill their head with details about the 5 litre, 32 valve V8 engine; concerned I might tell them how the 0-60 time is a shade over 6 seconds and that it max's out at nearly 180mph. And I understand that virtually no-one would be interested in the fact that the car develops 320bhp. That's OK, I don't care too much about that stuff.

But I do care about classic Porsches.

I was 12 when my friend, Neil McMath, introduced me to Porsches. Until that point, I was Porsche ambivalent; knew nothing of their existence. But I did recognise the cars he was pointing out and thought they looked pretty. So I got more and more interested and, once I looked into the story of the Porsche family, the company, it's place in world and car history, I started to really sit up and pay attention.

From then on, I devoured whatever information about these cars I could. I would watch and re-watch Risky Business, crying the first time the 928 went in the lake (idiot). I wrote to all the local garages who were kind enough to fill this fledgeling Porschephile's hands with the brochures of the day. More material. Unlike the Ferraris and Lambourghinis of the day, you could drive a Porsche to the racetrack, spend all day zooming around, then pop to the shops in it. The Ferraris and Lambos were, inevitably, at the side of the track with steam pouring out of every orifice.

Fact.

I got my first Porsche in my early 20s. A scary moment. After all, these were potential money pits if you buy a wrong one. Thankfully, my first 944 was a right one. It was beautiful, lovely to drive, quick enough and clearly quality. It suited me to a tee.

I kept that car for many years. I still had it when I met Vikki. I would like to say that she was impressed, but I'd not yet introduced her into the Porsche club. ("She will learn though, oh yes, she will...")

Once we dug ourselves out of our first major financial hell, we found ourselves in the position to get a turbo-charged version of the 944. It was a no-brainer. Sadly, this car *was* the aforementioned money pit and, after spending as much on repairs as we had on the car initially, we sold it.

Then followed a sojourn into a slightly different kind of motoring. A Daimler DS420 hearse. This was right at the beginning of SLT's notoriety and it really helped get the band known. We had it sign written in SLT livery and to say it got attention where it went would be like saying that Bill Gates has a quid or two. It worked, well.

However, all good things must come to an end and, after many years happy motoring, the hearse met it's own maker at the breakers yard in the sky. It was time to go back to the Porsche stable and we picked up a black 944.

We kept that car for about five years. It was 100% reliable in that time and didn't really have a reason to sell. But we were keeping half an eye out for something else. It was during one of these half-eyes that Vikki spotted a 928 on eBay, in bright yellow. A very unusual colour for these cars, one that made it both unique and stunning.

It didn't meet the reserve, so Vikki called and made a cheeky offer, which included the part exchange of our 944. It was accepted!

A moment more terrifying than my initial Porsche purchase followed. The 928 is an incredible car, if you don't buy a dog. If you do buy a dog, expect to sell everything you own – including the dog – to pay for it. HT leads, for example - simple HT leads - nearly £400. And, yes, we did have to buy some during our ownership.

That ownership was a pleasure. An expensive pleasure. It is one of those cars you forgive though, as soon as you sit in it and press the loud pedal. I was in love, hook, line and sinker. This was a £90k car in 1989 and still felt awesome today.

As far as I was concerned, this was it. I was keeping this car for ever, putting it through a rolling restoration to make it in A1 condition, whilst enjoying it for everything it was worth. A great investment too, as the prices are headed skyward. If you had told me that I would one day voluntarily sell that car, I would have smacked you upside the head with the wheel jack, before wheel spinning on your clearly teeny, tiny brain.

Yet, I did sell it. I didn't need the money and it has left me a bit confused and bemused, with a little hole in my heart.. I sold it not happily, but willingly.

So, what the hell could have happened for this complete volte face to have taken place?

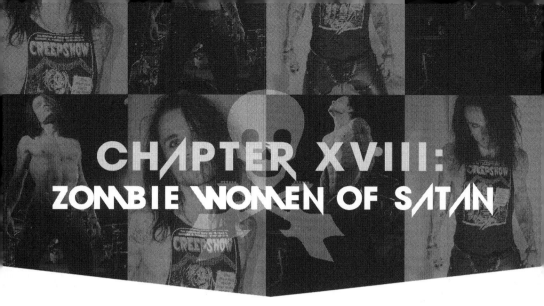

CHAPTER XVIII:
ZOMBIE WOMEN OF SATAN

O ne of the perks of being in a band is that your music is
sometimes wanted for movies. This was the first time,
however, that we had been asked to actually appear in a
film. An exciting opportunity, not to be missed.

Being shot in Newcastle, it was almost at the other end of the country
but we were quite determined to do this. The film, Zombie Women
Of Satan 2 was, as the name might suggest, the sequel to a cult movie
often shown on the Horror Channel. Apart from the excitement of
appearing in a film, I thought it could also be extremely good for our
international prospects.

Our role in the film was simple: play ourselves. We can do that, no
problem, so arrived on set at the allotted time and placed all our gear on
the requested stage. We'd not seen the script so weren't entirely certain
what to expect – whether we were miming or playing live – and what
the actual scene entailed.

I loved the buzz of being on a film set, even a small indie
production like this one. The cast, crew and extras filling every other
corner; the equipment; the rest! Anyone that has been on a film set
knows there is a lot of waiting around and this was no exception, so
I spent a lot of time just absorbing the atmosphere and the general
goings-on. I liked it. A lot.

Then we were up. We had to perform one of our songs as though we were the house band at a disco. We would play it live for the first couple of takes, just to get the vibe right and then we would mime to playback. As the takes wore on and the scene progressed, we had to pretend to play in absolute silence. It was very strange, watching a silent audience "scream" whilst we rocked as hard as possible. Silently. It was good fun though and we were in hysterics, timing our giggles for the moments the camera was pointing in the opposite direction.

I was watching the director, Warren Speed. He had also written the film, produced it and was starring in it. I had read about him in a recent issue of Skin Deep so was aware of him and his activities, which is why I didn't need to think twice about helping out. I was impressed with the whole movie set up and his devotion to it, but I was also struck by the fact that he wasn't doing anything that I didn't think I could do myself. He was just kind of bossing people around, organising things, performing, making small adjustments, shifting people, trying things a different way. In other words, what I had been doing for the past 10 years as the "leader" of the band.

It was a long drive home. Still fuelled with adrenaline, I found it easy. I used the time to think about the day, how much I had enjoyed it and how much I would love to do that kind of thing on a regular basis. It felt exotic. I guess in the same way people look at bands and just see the glossy surface - failing to understand the thousands of hours of hard work it took to get to that point – I was looking at the movie business through those same, rose tinted glasses.

I wanted in and was going to do what I could to get us in more movies. Little did I realise at the time quite where this new ambition would lead. It wouldn't be too long before I was to find out.

CHAPTER XIX:
FEAR OF FLYING

An achievement of which I am mightily proud is overcoming my fear of flying. To say it was phobic is an understatement. It was debilitating. There was absolutely NO WAY that I was ever going to get on an aeroplane, even though I desperately wanted to easily reach the places air travel can take you.

It was also not particularly helpful for the music career. In the past, I had actually turned down good opportunities because flying was involved. Of course, at the time, I justified it to myself by pretending that it wasn't viable for some reason or another, but this was not always true.

If ever I dreamt of flying, it was always a dream filled with terror and dread. A nightmare. I was always taken away against my will, somewhat Mr T like. I couldn't comprehend how people would willingly board one of these aluminium death traps. Clearly, they were fucking morons.

How did this fear start? When did it manifest itself? I have tried to analyse this, especially as I had flown many times before, as a child. The last flight I took was when I was 14 years old, to Majorca, with my parents. I had never had a bad experience on a plane and had never been overly concerned about air travel. I didn't like my ears popping, but who does?

One thing I do remember is that my mum would wear a St Christopher medal – the patron saint of travel. I must have found this a bit suspicious and it must have seeped into my subconscious somewhere; the implication being that a successful flight was more of an act of God than an act of Physics.

As an adult, I was always too skint to consider a holiday. Then I had all my aforementioned concerns over death. My belief is that my overwhelming desire to avoid death, or potentially death-defying situations, made me rule out flying. I didn't need to do it and, if anything went wrong, you are pretty much done for. It wasn't until my early 20s that I realised I had this fear, when a friend offered me a free trip to Brussels and I refused to go.

Many years passed and the fear became part of the psyche. I still couldn't afford to holiday and figured I could take a boat if necessary to tour. Then I got serious. Or, rather, the band got serious and I realised I needed to do something about this fear or give up any dreams of travelling the globe as an international rock star.

Every now and again, I had been tempted by the Fear Of Flying courses that some forward thinking airlines run. I was going to do it. We had the money to book me on the course and I was just going to DO IT.

Then that sodding Icelandic volcano exploded, grounding all flights, including the one at the end of the Fear of Flying course. Bollocks. Course cancelled. This might not have been the end of the world if I hadn't agreed to play the first Hard Rock Hell Ibiza festival. Why did I agree to that? Well, because we had played Hard Rock Hell in the UK and got on well with the organisers, the illogical part of my brain told me that "they wouldn't let anything bad happen to me". The mind is an odd thing, at times.

So, what to do? Vikki suggested just booking a random flight. It seemed like an idea so I chose Guernsey, the place I had flown to and from more times in my life than anywhere else. Maybe as many as 10 return journeys as a child. Again, anti-logic played it's part: I knew it to be fact that I had flown safely before to Guernsey, so I felt a sense of comfort in that. It was also a short flight.

Surprisingly, I did actually get a little bit of sleep the night before, but that is not to say I wasn't nervous. I was terrified and this was a baby-steps moment. It felt like I was on a conveyor belt, heading toward this destination whether I liked it or not. That was probably a good mindset to help as it stopped me turning and running.

"Everything is OK right now." That is what I kept telling myself. I just needed a whole heap of those together and I would be safe. I wasn't going into this totally blind, I don't think I could have. Education is power and, prior to flying, I learned what I could about the physics of flight, what inherent risks there are (or, more importantly, aren't) and what I could expect from the flight: from the physical sensations to the noises the aircraft might make. Armed with this information made me stronger.

It helped me enormously on the flight. I knew to expect a large "clunk" sound when the landing gear retracted. I understood that there is an odd sensation of barely moving when the plane slows in the air. Best of all, I knew that, even if all the engines stopped, the plane wouldn't – couldn't – just fall out of the sky. The laws of physics simply do not allow it. I was quietly confident.

The plane was tiny. A little propeller job with the teeniest seats imaginable. I have slim hips but it was tight for me. No matter. Thankfully, Vikki is small and didn't mind my elbows. Taxiing down the runway, I was wondering what the hell I was doing, but I was also experiencing surges of adrenaline and excitement. Was I really about to do this? Well, yeah, I was strapped in so it was totally out of my control now.

We lifted off. I was shitting a brick. But only for the first thirty seconds. As we soared skyward; as I watched the houses shrink and the fields turn into a patchwork cloth draped over rolling hills; I was left

TAXIING DOWN THE RUNWAY, I WAS WONDERING WHAT THE HELL I WAS DOING, BUT I WAS ALSO EXPERIENCING SURGES OF ADRENALINE AND EXCITEMENT. WAS I REALLY ABOUT TO DO THIS? WELL, YEAH, I WAS STRAPPED IN SO IT WAS TOTALLY OUT OF MY CONTROL NOW."

only feeling excitement. And wonder. Total wonder. And awe. Damn us humans are a clever bunch. Why had I denied myself this for so long?

I was hooked. That flight, and the one home later that day, were brilliant, as was the flight a month or so later to Ibiza. Since then, I have flown 18 more times or so. That may not be a lot to some but, for someone that never ever thought he could, let alone would, get on a plane, it is something short of a miracle.

Except it isn't a miracle. It is understanding that most fear is borne of ignorance. I was ignorant to the experience of flight and how it actually works. By overcoming that ignorance and educating myself, I gave myself the control back.

It was one of the biggest learning curves of my life so far, and one of the proudest moments.

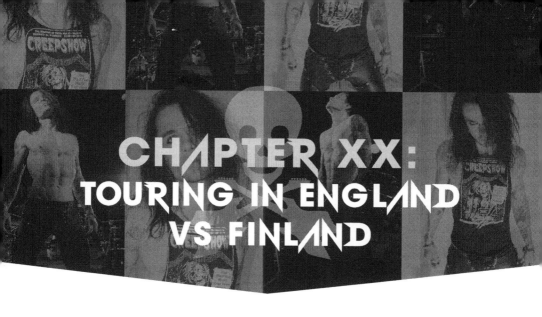

CHAPTER XX:
TOURING IN ENGLAND
VS FINLAND

The final quarter of 2012 saw us embark on a tour of the UK and a small blast in Finland. The differences were quite staggering. Tours are always a bit stressful. Lots to organise prior; schedules to keep during; as well as trying to remain as rested, fit and healthy as possible to give a good performance. I had always found them tough, being the driver, and it didn't help that our drummer had to be cajoled into helping out in any way possible. As per usual, Vikki and I did most of the legwork in organising before and the physical labour during.

But this was what I wanted, right? A life on the road? Travelling from city to city to entertain a neighbourhood before blasting off to uncharted territory to do it all over again? I was seriously beginning to have my doubts. Day one of the tour didn't help much.

The first venue, The Hallcross in Doncaster. That was a helluva long drive back then, so it was a relief to get there. We unloaded into the pub venue and waited for someone to tell us where to set up, where to put our overnight stuff and who was doing the sound for the night.

It isn't usual to stay in the venue over night but our T&Cs stipulated accommodation. A cheap hotel was usually provided. However, the Hallcross insisted that they had accommodation and, whilst not pretending it to be luxury, they did at least suggest that it was liveable. They fucking lied.

You have never, in your life, seen such a cesspit. If you have backpacked around India, you won't have encountered deprivation like it. OK, slight exaggeration for comedic effect, but it was shocking. There was dirty laundry everywhere. Boxes full of personal effects. It was the worst kind of unclean, the kind of place where you daren't eat anything as you would absolutely, definitely catch cooties. Or worse. As for the kitchen? If they had smeared dog shit over the work surfaces, it would have improved things. The fridge still had contents, contents that had not been cleared since the early 80s by the looks of things, and the mould ran amok throughout.

We were going to have to try and sleep in this pig sty.

Ah well, at least we had the fun of the gig first. At least there was that. Well, we would do if the sound guy showed up. Playing a gig without a PA is tricky, to say the least. The Hallcross "forgot" to book anyone so, when we showed up (which appeared to be a surprise to them) they got on the phone behind our backs, in a panic, to find someone.

Eventually, a rather dishevelled looking person arrived with a PA, so at least we would be able to make a bit of noise now.

Things were looking up. It is amazing, when you hit rock bottom, anything positive becomes the Best Thing Ever. On this day, it was the food which was catered by an Italian restaurant nearby. Very nice it was too.

Back to the chaos.

We asked about promotion. We always sent up flyers and posters, expecting the venue to at least stick them on their wall so regulars know that we are coming. We couldn't see any around, however, so we were beginning to sweat. Lucky for us, the Hallcross were one step ahead and promotion was underway: a hastily hand-written chalk board stuck outside the venue half an hour before we were due to play. YES, I AM BEING FUCKING SARCASTIC.

To say that our hearts weren't in it that evening is an understatement. The few that did show were treated to a sub-par, short set. Usually, when a low turnout occurs, you can rise above it and still put on a show but, this being the first gig, it felt like a portent of things to come. So ashamed was I of the situation we were in, I played a lot of the gig with my back to the audience; I couldn't face them. I haven't done that since my earliest shows when I would do it out of nerves.

When it was over, I still couldn't face anyone. I was polite as I could be in the circumstances, made my excuses and retired to my room. I made a small attempt to tidy it. There was no bed, so I cleared a space on the floor (barely) and laid down a grubby mattress. I found some dirty sheets and resigned myself to sleeping fully clothed. This was not my fault, yet I felt myself feeling bad for putting Vikki through this. She was suffering because she was following me on this crazy mission. I know that wasn't the case, but at that moment, I was racked with guilt.

Just as we laid our heads down on the (dirty) pillow, two girls walked in. Who the hell these were, we had no idea. Apparently though, we were sleeping in their rooms! Un-fucking-believable. Well, there was NO way that we were budging as there wasn't anywhere else we could go. We pretty much kicked them out and closed the door in their faces. Where they slept, I neither know nor care.

Laying there, having suffered the indignity of the days' events, I really was questioning WHY. I'd had these thoughts before, but I was really vocal about them this time. I was a 40 year old man, sleeping rough on the floor of a shitty pub after playing possibly the worst gig of my life. The why's were coming at me thick and fast. I said to Vikki that I wasn't sure if I could continue with the tour, let alone anything beyond that. She talked sense into me and I fell into a fitted sleep.

Next day, I did feel a bit brighter. I have a knack of being able to leave the previous days' troubles behind and I was in fighting mood. We got the fuck out of Doncaster as quick as we could, onto the next venue. That night's accommodation was great and most of the gigs that followed were brilliant, a couple our best ever. Still, something wasn't sitting right with me. I couldn't work out if I was enjoying this any more.

It was the next month that we flew to Finland for three shows. Collected from the airport by our hosts, we were taxied in relative luxury (with the support band) to our hotel. It wasn't plush, but it was warm, clean and comfortable and made a happy temporary home.

Being winter, there was a lot of snow and it was great fun being ferried around and not having the concern of the drive. It was someone else's responsibility and that really took the pressure off me. Despite the tour happening during our business' busiest time, it was almost relaxing.

The shows were fun, too. We were fed and watered, our rider taken care of as best it could be, always kept informed of events and someone was always at hand to help out. Only there for three days but we would have happily stayed longer. The Saturday night gig in Helsinki remains one of the best memories I have of touring. It really felt like an adventure. For that fleeting trip, all was right with the world of rock n' roll again. Even the comical farce of dumb and dumber (our nick name for Gilez and Rob; drums and guitar) nearly missing their flight home could only be laughed at and mocked for all it was worth.

I finished the year on a high, trying to forget the night at the Hallcross best I could and focussing my energies on the good gigs and the overseas shenanigans. If we could have less of the former and more of the latter, perhaps we could get this thing to work out. Perhaps.

CHAPTER XXI:
A PRIME EXAMPLE OF STUPIDITY OR A FIERCE INDEPENDENT STREAK?

T hroughout the writing of this book, which is an exercise in trying to understand how I became the man I am and what to do about it, I am often reminded of events that seem like they happened to somebody else. Sadly, they happened to me and, in all cases, were down to my own volition.

There are many examples to choose from and it was a toss up between the time I advertised myself as a children's entertainer getting booked to do a fifth birthday party, and the time I had an operation. Granted, the former is more rife for comic hilarity, but no lesson can be learned from it other than I was A Bit Mental. The operation also suggests that I was A Bit Mental, but also that I was extreme in asserting my independence.

When my parents pretty much washed their hands of me after I announced I wanted to pursue a career in music, I realised that I was on my own. Don't get me wrong, they didn't want harm to come to me and I understand that their stance was out of fear. *That old nemesis again*. They feared I wouldn't "make it" so, rather than support my desire to at least try, they attempted to force me into a position to back down. Clearly, this wasn't going to happen, so we had a turbulent few years.

Since then, they have changed – something they credit to watching me follow my own path – and we are one big happy family again.

But this is not what this chapter is about. This chapter is about an operative procedure I had when I was about 19 or 20. It was a cosmetic surgery to rectify a nature given "gift" that I called puffy nipples but is known in the medical profession as Gynecomastia (I still reckon my term is better). It is extremely common in boys who get it during puberty as a surge in hormones causes all sorts of odd imbalances, the glands under the nipples temporarily swell, causing them to jut out and lose their stuck limpet look.

For years, I presumed that my puffy nipples were something to do with my weight. Knowing about how fat affects the body now, I may have been onto something as increased weight does cause an increase in the female hormone, oestrogen, and it was this bad girl that was causing my issue. However, when I lost weight at 18 and became the proverbial rake, my nipples stuck out like they were attached to charging rhinos, so this was clearly a problem that wasn't going away.

Off I went to the doctor who confirmed that it was unlikely this would go away by itself (I had had it many years by this point) so it was agreed that I could have surgery on the NHS as it caused me mental anguish. Good news.

When the date came through, it was several years hence. As I was hyper sensitive to my nipples – wearing double layers of clothing to press them down and NEVER going topless – this caused me great misery, so I went to my grandparents for help. They agreed to lend me the money to go private, the not inconsiderable sum of £1,900.

I did not tell any of my family when the surgery was due. I didn't want my parent's pity or concern as, to me, it seemed incongruous to their recent behaviour. At least that is what I thought at the time, now looking back, I realise it is just because I am a right stubborn little bastard.

I was also not prepared to go fully under anaesthesia. My mum had known a school friend die during an op and her concerns (and recollection of that story whenever anyone was going to have an operation) made me very wary of it. Couple that with me hating the idea of my consciousness being taken away from me, there was no way it was going to happen.

The operating surgeon was not happy but, I was paying the bill, so he went along with it. I would have local anaesthetic injected into each nipple – a prospect I was not exactly looking forward to – but would be conscious throughout.

This was the first time I felt that inevitable walk along the gang plank and I took the same baby steps I would adopt later in my life as I boarded that comeback plane ride. I had refused to take my jewellery off (I was a cool rock star, had to look the part) and was laying on the gurney awaiting the first injection. As it happens, it didn't hurt anywhere near as much as anticipated and it wasn't long before I was aware of a numbness across my chest.

I could tell the surgeon was pissed at me when he started jabbing the needle into my nipples asking if I could feel anything. I could not and was, by this point, delightfully off my tits (pun intended) on whatever it is they pump you full of. *That was it, I was going to watch.* So, I moved the little curtain they had made out of the sheet and tried to view what was going on.

They cut a semi circle around each nipple, then folded it inside out to reveal the gland. This was then chopped out and I was stitched up, leaving a little gap for a tube to drain fluids. The first one went great, the second one, not so good. I don't know if they fucked up or if it was my fidgeting, it just wasn't as neat and tidy. It didn't help that I was chatting up the nurses from my clearly very sexy position (laying on the bed with my boobs cut open). It also didn't help that I informed the surgeon, whilst he was in me, that he was "not much better than a murderer", my logic being that the only difference was that he was allowed to cut people.

I had a way of endearing myself to others, back then.

When it was over, I was wheeled back into my room. Going private meant that I had a little suite of my own with food on offer: prawns and steak. There was also a little button which, whenever I pressed it, a nurse would appear like magic. I saw a lot of that nurse for the hour I stayed. But then I got restless and bored and decided to leave. This was against advice but I didn't much care. My chest was strapped up with the tightest elasticated medical bandage; I had two tubes draining ooze from my boobs and I was still completely off my trolley.

So I drove home. Somehow, I managed to dress myself with the one hand I was able to kind of move, signed myself out and got into the car. The drive home was harrowing. My left arm was the one that was working, but the tightness of the bandage meant that movement was restricted. Each gear change was a real physical effort, along with a fine dalliance between steering, clutch, brake and paying attention to the road. All whilst being under the influence of whatever wonder drug they had pumped me full of.

I made it home, via a quick visit to my parents to guilt-trip them. The journey had not been easy, navigating twisting country roads and the seatbelt had rubbed my right nipple. Unfortunately, this was the one they had had trouble with.

I got home to my house-mate playing very loud guitar through his brand new Marshall amp. I told him to shut the fuck up and went to my room, feeling a bit under the weather by now.

My sickness increased throughout the day and the pain under my right nipple was becoming unbearable as the drugs wore off. I have a high tolerance for pain and a low tolerance for hospitals, so it surprised everyone when I accepted an offer to be driven, at midnight, to the emergency room.

A very pissed off surgeon arrived, complaining that it was my fault and that I had knocked out the little tube that drained fluids. My wounds had begun to heal, sealing the fluids underneath, giving myself some lovely blood poisoning, hence my sickness. He rather unceremoniously squeezed my chest like the biggest pimple. To add to the pimple analogy, it burst under pressure and I felt warm liquid puss dribble down my sides. It was fucking gross.

Next day, I had to return. This time, I allowed my mum and dad to take me. Yes, I knew I was invincible but, on this rare occasion, the comfort of my parents being there didn't seem so bad.

CHAPTER XXII:
2013 - NORWAY: THE SEQUEL

We started 2013 with another trip to Norway. This one was slightly different though, as it was to shoot a film. After the "Zombie Women Of Satan 2" adventure, I had been keeping an eye out for other movie opportunities when I saw a casting call for a film set in Norway. I answered it and almost immediately got a positive response. A bonus of being in quite a well-known band is that our names can bring attention to indie projects.

Oddly enough, the film was being made by a guy that lived over the road from my parents. A few years younger than me, we didn't hang out as kids but did remember each other. Such a small world! So, Vikki and I signed up to appear in "Blaze Of Gory: Snow", part of an anthology of films based on the writings of a rather disturbed 12 year old girl.

It was only a small unit heading out to Norway: me, Vikki, David (director) and Duff, another actor and soon-to-be driver. We were going to meet the only other cast member, Susie, out in Norway. She was flying in from New York.

6am is never a great call-time but, hey, we were excited. Not often you get to play these kinds of games. Met David and Duff at Gatwick and, before long, were on the plane bound for Norway.

We met Susie at Oslo airport then collected the hire car. I am a nervous passenger but Duff assured me he would drive slowly and, true to his word, he did. There was a lot of snow around and I didn't want us skidding everywhere. We first headed to a town about 30 minutes from our final destination to get some supplies. I remember sitting on tables by a café, checking the internet, excited about the day so far and looking forward to the evening. If only I'd have known...

The rest of the journey went well. To a point. That point being about a mile away from our location for three days: a cabin in the woods. It was going up a slight hill that the car hit some ice, skidded to a jaunty sideways position, wedging itself between the two verges. One side was a sheer rock face going up, the other a sheer drop into woods. The snow was deep, it was -25° outside and we were stuck 30 miles from the nearest town.

At first, we were laughing away at our predicament. You know how it is, these things happen and, within a few moments, we'll be out of there. But it was not to be.

We spent five hours sitting at that bit of the road, contemplating our future. I genuinely had the thought "I am not going to bloody die in this car in the middle of woods in Norway". Not that I was scared, more that it seemed to be a distinct possibility. After all, once the diesel ran out, we would have been unable to have run the car, which was our only source of heat. We'd then have to start setting fire to eachother. David and Duff did suggest that they go and try to find the cabin but the combination of pitch darkness, snow and ice, meant that the tiniest error could easily have proved fatal. Plus they would be the first we'd burn.

Eventually, we decided to start calling the Police. After all, this was an emergency. I cannot quite remember the exact sequence of events but we were ultimately rescued by a man in a tow truck with "Viking"

 I GENUINELY HAD THE THOUGHT "I AM NOT GOING TO BLOODY DIE IN THIS CAR IN THE MIDDLE OF WOODS IN NORWAY". NOT THAT I WAS SCARED, MORE THAT IT SEEMED TO BE A DISTINCT POSSIBILITY."

written on the side. He was a bit of a grumpy bugger and didn't see the funny side at all. I don't know why, he was going to be paid, after all.

Once he towed us to a road where we could gain traction, we gingerly drove to the nearest town and started to try and find somewhere to lay our bones for the night. By this time, it was about 2am. David was freaking as we were supposed to shoot some scenes in the cabin today. Clearly, that wasn't going to happen and it was also beginning to look like we weren't going to find anywhere with rooms.

£400 was the going rate for the two rooms we did get. Granted, it was a great hotel but, seeing as we were only in it from 4am until about 10, we didn't get the most use out of it. Did I mention that Norway is fucking expensive? Fucking.

Next morning - after removing the parking ticket from the windscreen - we set off to try and find some snow chains for the tyres. You'd have thought the hire company might have provided them but, no, they did not. It took us a surprising amount of time to find the right ones, but find them we did and we headed back to the ice covered road.

At the bottom of the hill, D&D fitted the snow chains. We made it up the hill – passing our temporary parking spot en route – and continued to the cabin. No denying, it was gorgeous. A perfect log cabin, surrounded by fir trees, adjacent to a frozen lake, crested with a foot of snow. It was like Narnia.

We all agreed that David and Duff would most certainly have perished if they had attempted to find this place, so were all glad that Vikki had put her foot down. It was to be Vikki's role of general life saver for this trip, an attribute for which we are all truly grateful. And alive.

Once loaded into the cabin, we looked for devices to make heat and light. There was a wood burning stove and a couple of electric light switches. Putting them in the "on" position provided us with enough light to see an inch in front of our faces for about 20 seconds. They then went out and we discovered the power source was a car battery, connected to a solar panel on the roof, with six inches of snow atop.

So electricity wasn't happening, then.

And neither was heat. Us boys were making valiant attempts at fire, throwing everything onto it we could find. Lucky for us, Vikki was there and she took charge whilst I bravely went and sat in the car with the heat on. As cold as it was outside, it was just as cold in.

Finally, someone came out to me with a cup of hot chocolate (gas oven, thank fuck, that Vikki had also got working) and informed me that the wood burner was fully operational, thanks to "Bear Girls".

Damnit though, it was bloody cold. After several hours, we were still in minus figures. We did soldier on, however, and a few shots were made that night.

Without electricity, water, light or an indoor loo, this was not luxury accommodation. Clearly we were mad English people being typically, well, English and bloody stupid. But, you know what? It was alright. It was better than alright. Surrounded by such beauty and doing something interesting made the conditions somehow bearable. Enjoyable, even.

The next day was all action. It was to be the only full day we had as we were returning the day after. That meant filming a whole film – albeit a short – in one day. Unbelievably, because everyone chipped in, we did it. We even discovered how to make much heat with the lighting of many candles. At one point, it was so hot, we had to open the door!

It was one of those bonding experiences I don't think any of us will forget. Being in such close quarters in such extremities can bring out the worse in people but, you know what, we all got on the whole time and, in those few days, became friends for life. It was, in a word, Brilliant.

Little did I know at the time, that it would prepare me for things to come.

CHAPTER XXIII: NORMALITYVILLE HORROR, THE MOVIE

During the very rare periods of downtime in Norway, I grabbed David to spend some moments telling him about a movie idea I had been working on since November. So far, I was just fleshing out the story but, when I laid out the bare bones to him, he said that it sounded interesting and encouraged me to finish it.

I had already started reading books on writing screenplays: there is a lot to learn if you are starting without a clue. They need to be in a particular format, the beats should appear at certain points and, being prose-free, you have to re-think how you write. For example, in a book, a character can think – we can hear their thought processes. In a screenplay, you do not (unless that is a deliberate device of the narrative).

After David's words of encouragement - and once home with the frostbite abating - I set about writing "Normalityville Horror: The Movie". Why the same title as our recent CD? Well, why not? I thought it was a great title and, to me, it means some kind of dystopian future, which is something that fascinates me. I wanted to write my version of 1984, so that is what I did.

It took me a long time. Reading back on it now, I didn't get the formatting quite right. I did use some prose here and there but, that's

OK, it was a first attempt. The story is good and I like the characters, so I am almost there. Let's rewind back to the writing... It was hard. But not as hard as I thought it would be. On the whole, I found hitting the beats at the correct parts of the story a very natural thing to do. My exposition was nice, not the clumsy affair that you so often witness in films these days, and the story was an intricate one, that kept the reader – ultimately, viewer – guessing, right until the end. I also cannily left it open for a sequel, should it ever get made and be successful enough.

What took me one paragraph above to explain, took nearly six months to complete from the very first notes back in November. I didn't start writing it until I had digested many books, by different authors, on screenwriting. Some things made sense and I adopted them, others did not so I ignored them. Not that I think I know better, but because, wherever rules exist, they are there to be broken or, at the very least, challenged.

Nervously, I would let Vikki read each scene as I wrote it. She reads a lot of fiction (whereas I do not) so I felt her opinion would be an honest one as to whether it was any good. Or at least part way there. She too encouraged me to continue, so I did. Each day she wanted to read more, to find out what happened next, which made me eager to get on with it. I discovered that I loved to write and create these people and their world.

I have rarely been as satisfied as I was the day I finished writing it, printed it out and bound it. I was holding in my hand a fully-fledged screenplay. A film yet to be shot. A piece of cinema to be. *And I wrote it.* Six months earlier, the notion of writing a film seemed unlikely at best, impossible at worst. Yet, here I was with it, finished.

 I HAVE RARELY BEEN AS SATISFIED AS I WAS THE DAY I FINISHED WRITING IT, PRINTED IT OUT AND BOUND IT. I WAS HOLDING IN MY HAND A FULLY-FLEDGED SCREENPLAY. A FILM YET TO BE SHOT. A PIECE OF CINEMA TO BE. AND I WROTE IT."

Excitedly, I took a copy to David. I wanted him to be the first – after Vikki – to read it. From the look on his face, he was impressed that I had actually done it. I guess a lot of people say things, but not many Do. I was hoping he might be able to help me out; the initial idea to shoot a trailer to try and get funding.

Buoyed by my achievement, I started to contact producers and literary agents. I didn't know what to expect so I was happy when my very first email had a positive response. I was to send in my first screenplay.

The positive responses slowed down to about 1 in 10 emails. That was fine, I was used to that from being in music so long. There were several moments of elation, like when the Iron Sky producers requested a copy.

To-date, no-one has bitten. Truth be told, I only got a few responses back and they were all of the "good luck" variety. I am not disheartened, though. I have read enough to know that it can sometimes take years – decades – for films to get made. Besides, I have not been actively pursuing it for nearly 24 months now. You will find out why in the following chapters. Hopefully you won't be too disappointed in this temporary hiatus.

CHAPTER XXIV:
WHY I QUIT DRINKING

When I was 15, I was introduced to an adult in his 30s who was a nice guy. Until he drank, then he became a bit of an arse. He also fell asleep a lot and pissed himself. I thought this was pretty gross so, at that monumentally young age, I declared myself teetotal.

I remained that way until I was 22. Nothing in particular made me start drinking, other than the feeling that I might be missing out on something. I remember that day like it was yesterday: upon deciding that I would un-quit, I drove to a nearby shopping parade and purchased a couple of bottles of 20-20. I took them home, drank them both almost immediately and promptly threw up before passing out.

This did not seem to put me off and I spent the next few years drinking heavily when I could afford it. Then, the unthinkable happened. Some stupid bank gave me a credit card with a £10,000 limit. No fucking clue why but, it is safe to say, nearly every penny of that ten grand was spent on getting completely rat arsed. Often, I would drive to the nearby snooker hall, chuck my card behind the bar and drink to my heart's content, playing pool. I probably then drove home. I was an idiot.

I was also an idiot when I met Vikki, and remained one for the prevailing years. Being in a band meant that people are very eager to buy you drinks and share their drugs with you. Clearly, this was Awesome and I took advantage of it. A lot. I was never into beer, only spirits and I would pre-drink on the train before the "proper" drinking took place.

Obviously, there were fun times. There always is before things get dark. Like the time I was backstage at a Steve Vai concert, arse up in the air, insisting that Mr Vai bummed me. I then went outside, ingratiated myself with a homeless person, gave him all my money and cigarettes before attempting to move into his cardboard box. Thankfully, a friend found me and took me back to my non-cardboard-based abode.

Pretty soon though, the fun times became less and less and the dark clouds were gathering. Drinking when you have depressive issues is not a good thing. Apart from obscuring your judgement, it does nothing to help your brain and it could also cause you to make some pretty rash decisions. I know, I made quite a few.

The drinking got more and more, became heavier and heavier. We didn't have much money back then and drinking was now a daily necessity. I remember those feelings of panic when I thought I wouldn't be able to sooth my soul with booze that night. Somehow, we always managed to get some. Some of the most rancid, cheap shit you can imagine, but it got me pissed.

I was no longer drinking to have fun or to be social, I was drinking because I had to. My body had become accustomed to the regular intake of sugar and alcohol so I craved it daily, getting the DTs until I imbibed. I kid myself that it was all under control, it was rock n' roll but, fact of the matter is, I lost the tiny amount of control I may have once had.

Slowly, I saw myself as Death. I reflected this in my make-up and used to white-out my face, paint my eyes black and darken my cheekbones. I was trying to make my face look like a skull; reflecting on the outside what I felt like on the inside. All control had now evaporated and it was my mission to cause as much trouble as possible when caning it.

How I avoided serious injury, I don't quite know. I can only surmise that Vikki – who had essentially become my carer – was doing a much better job of looking after me than I was. Clearly, she was worried, but she also knew that she couldn't tell me what to do and I don't think she really knew what to do, other than try and prevent me from hurting myself too seriously.

Looking back, my drinking got so out of hand as I was masking the emotional pain I was in. I never dealt with the deaths of my nan or my granddad, preferring to reach for the bottle whenever I thought about them. Once I did get a grip and stopped, I was an emotional wreck for a while as I had to grieve, several years after the events.

I was also desperate for my dad to adopt me. When my sperm father left my mum and she re-married the person I call and think of as Dad, I took his last name and we acted as father and son. Knowing that trying to get permission for him to adopt me officially would be difficult, awkward and upsetting, it was something that we never did when I was a child. Now, more than anything, I wanted it to be official. He gave me a life I could never have had without him; along with love, stability *and* a little brother. I can never be his blood, but he is more important to me than most that are. He and my mum are on an equal footing for my affection and, if they want me to choose between them, the winner would have to bribe me, big time.

Vikki looked into the adoption thing for me but, surprise surprise, as someone in their 30s, adoption was no longer an option. This still makes me sad as there isn't much I want more than for him to adopt me, even today. The pain of this was often too much for me to bear and I would break down, smashing the place up before passing out among tears and shards of glass.

Clearly, this was not a sustainable situation. As well as the mental anguish that was out of control, I was deteriorating physically. Even the tiniest amount of alcohol made me feel hungover, sick, with a headache. My body was unable to process it. My kidneys hurt daily. I looked like hell and felt much worse.

I remember thinking, in one of my more lucid moments, that I was going to end up a lonely old man being a burden to my brother; living in a spare room of his with no money, no friends, drinking every day until he discovered my lifeless body. I didn't want to put that upon him and his family and it was not a future I wanted for myself. But, for some reason, I could not see a way out. That future seemed almost inevitable and stopping drinking seemed like the easiest thing in the world as an action, but the hardest thing as a mental challenge.

Then, one day, it happened. I still don't know where the strength came from. I suspect that my will to survive and thrive overcame everything else, forcing me into a corner. So it was, in May 2006, I had my last drink.

For a while, I went along to Alcoholic's Anonymous. I actually went a month or so after quitting to support my drummer, who had his own demons to overcome. He was inspired by my actions so we decided to try AA together. To be honest, I didn't think I was an alcoholic. In that first meeting though, I learned their definition of an alcoholic: someone whose life has become unmanageable because of alcohol. Well, this was me alright so I thought I had better pay attention.

Not to knock AA, but it ultimately was not for me. I find it has too much of a cultish vibe and seems to have a religious bent that does not sit well. I prefer to find strength in myself, from within, rather than from others, externally. To this day, over ten years later, I have still not had a drink.

How has this affected me? Well, it wasn't long before I started to feel and look a lot healthier. I mentioned the grieving I had to do – and some growing up – well, I got through it and came out the other side. That was probably the hardest bit, as the temptation was there when the pain increased. Vikki supported my action by quitting booze

DO I MISS DRINKING? SOMETIMES, YES. I DON'T THINK ABOUT IT MUCH, BUT WHEN I DO OCCASIONALLY THINK OF ONE OF MY FAVOURITE TIPPLES, I WONDER IF I COULD HAVE "JUST ONE", BUT I WON'T. I'M NOT SCARED OF IT ANY MORE, I JUST DON'T WANT IT IN MY LIFE."

herself. I don't know if I could have done it without that solidarity; I like to think yes, but maybe no.

I go from strength to strength. Every year without drinking is a year where I learn more about life and myself. I no longer hide from things in fear, I face them head on like a tough motherfucker. I still have weaknesses and issues, but I am aware of them and try to iron them out. I know I am not perfect and never will be, but I will try to build the best version of myself that I can.

Do I miss drinking? Sometimes, yes. I don't think about it much, but when I do occasionally think of one of my favourite tipples, I wonder if I could have "just one", but I won't. I'm not scared of it any more, I just don't want it in my life. I don't want the expense or the complications. I am better without it so, why would I? I certainly don't need it to enjoy myself or socialise; I am mentally stronger than most with a quick wit, so I like to have all my faculties with me at all times.

I most certainly wouldn't be able to cope with the events of 2014 as a piss artist, that's for sure.

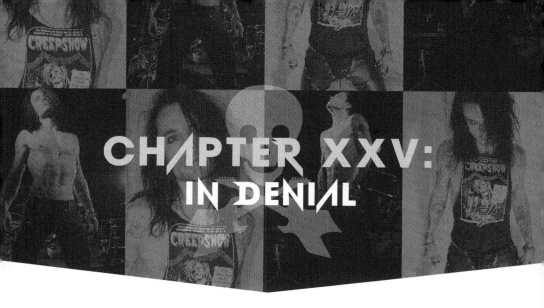

CHAPTER XXV:
IN DENIAL

L ife as I knew it carried on as expected during the first half of 2013. We had some live shows, pushing to get more, our CD came out in Europe, did the usual round of interviews and promo spots to try and let people know about it.

The only thing that was different was my enthusiasm. The last tour had been a real low-point for me; it felt like a turning point and, in hindsight, it was. Still, I didn't know for sure and we pursued our activities as a band lining up a couple of video shoots.

We shot two vids within a short space of time of each other - one in June, one in July – and I should really have known right then that something was up. One shoot made sense to film in the hall across the road from our house: it was low budget, was going to be messy and a controllable environment was a must. It went off as expected, was enormous fun and we got covered in copious amounts of blood. It was also a freebie, directed by my good man, David VG Davies, whom we had been to Norway with. Also on the shoot were Lucy and Craig. I had never met these two individuals before and was not to know what an important role they would play in my life, just a few months down the road.

When it came to the second shoot though, the one we were paying for, I really just couldn't be arsed. I had a conversation with the director beforehand and he was all for doing something quite elaborate that meant us travelling into London, having long days and so on. This sounded about as appealing as trying to remove dick cheese with a grater, so I came up with a much better plan that involved using the hall across the road from my house. In other words, I could barely muster up the energy for this video, so just roll me over there and I will do what I have to when asked.

As it turned out, it was an enjoyable day. It was also the wrong choice as that video never saw the light of day*. It was wrong. It was no good. It was a shit video. I blame myself for that, for being totally lazy. But I really just could not be bothered. Twelve months earlier, I was quite happy to spend a couple of days on a video shoot, many miles from home, with little sleep - but no longer. The effort-to-reward ratio was clearly very skewed as, whatever we did would be misused by the label and no fucker would get to see it anyway.

However, something good came out of it. I had a discussion with David (not that David, a different one: David Kenny AKA Johnny Crash) about low budget horror movies. He used to make them in the late nineties/early noughties in New York. He had been thinking about doing it again but needed someone to write them. I had written Normalityville Horror and was working on a comedy called Nazi Fun Park – perhaps one of these would work?

He loved them. But, they would be prohibitively expensive to make, so I thought about toning down the production. I thought about a subject that was popular: Zombies. I thought about a British film series that was popular: The Carry On films and I started writing "Zombies Go Camping".

 IT WAS A SHIT VIDEO. I BLAME MYSELF FOR THAT, FOR BEING TOTALLY LAZY. BUT I REALLY JUST COULD NOT BE BOTHERED. TWELVE MONTHS EARLIER, I WAS QUITE HAPPY TO SPEND A COUPLE OF DAYS ON A VIDEO SHOOT, MANY MILES FROM HOME, WITH LITTLE SLEEP - BUT NO LONGER."

Within 10 days, I was finished. I had written a warm, funny film that got really intense and scary. It focussed around a family of friendly zombies, the Cadavers. At the heart of the film is a loving family who go camping, only to find the human campers prejudiced against them. Some nasty twists of fate see them save the day and win the humans over. It is a tale of bullying, overcoming adversity, growing up and family.

It is also a scary as-all-shit slasher movie.

David loved it and wanted to do it. The title changed to the much more inspired "Meet The Cadavers" and I set about trying to put the wheels in motion. And this was when David hit the brakes. However much he would love to do something, it wouldn't be able to be this side of 2013. I, on the other hand, was itching to start. It was late July and, if we didn't do it in the next couple of months, we would lose the weather and the daylight hours delaying us until Spring.

He was unmoveable, so I looked for a Plan B.

Meanwhile, I was cancelling gigs left, right and centre. Some of them naturally fell by the wayside, as is often the case, but here I was coming up with any and every excuse under the sun to cancel a gig. This was a state of play that continued until February 2014. I just didn't want to be up there, but I didn't want to admit that to myself, let alone anyone else.

*   This video has since been released. Later you will learn of my editing "prowess". Well, I put that to good use and made a few changes to the clip that enhanced it enough for it to be seen. So, go to www.youtube.com/spitlikethis and search for the song "Sick".

CHAPTER XXVI:
MEET THE CADAVERS

A note from the author: It is here where chronology must take over. We have explored my past, have some background and information that helps explain my personality, along with some of the choices I have made. After the gradual ascent of my band from inception to 2010, I have documented it's slow demise whilst grappling with the physical and mental changes that occur over time. As my interest in one form of artistic expression waned, others piqued my interest. All the events that follow will maybe go to explain why I am sitting here a bit bemused, lacking clarity as to what my next moves should be.

B ack in late Summer 2013 though, it was very clear. I was going to make a fucking movie whether anyone liked it or not. David Kenny wouldn't or couldn't do it, so I turned to David Davies. Although the original plan to make lo-fi horrors was with David K, I saw no reason why I shouldn't do it with Mr Davies instead.

So, I gave him a call and sent him the script. I won't deny it, I was nervous. With his involvement, this film would get made. Without it, it could get made, but fuck only knows when. And how. Thankfully, I did not have to wait long for his reply: "This has to be made". Awesome. A meeting was hastily set up where he explained to me the early stages of pre-production and we wrote big lists of what we would need to do before we shot a second of film. It was a long and daunting list, especially to someone that was only just learning some of the terminology (let alone the ropes), but I knew David would guide me through it.

Then the unthinkable happened: David lost his mum. It wasn't unexpected, but it obviously hit him hard. I didn't want any extra pressure to fall on his shoulders so I took it upon myself to do as much of the pre-production as I possibly could.

I placed adverts for cast and crew, answering all replies and viewing all audition videos. I went through the script to determine every single prop, location and special effect that would be required. I liaised with Lucy (from the video shoot) over the Cadaver's make-up. I designed and shopped for wardrobe for all the characters and went prop hunting. I contacted companies to try and blag free gear. I traipsed around the south east, visiting numerous camp sites, doing recces to find the perfect locations. I negotiated and rang and emailed. I met with cast and crew, auditioning young actors. I compiled scene lists and shot lists and worked out who needed to be where and when. I could go on. And on and on.

We had set a start date of 19th October 2013. A little later than I had wanted, but we were experiencing an Indian Summer, so hopefully that would hold. Shooting would be done over 5 weekends throughout October, November and December. The whole thing was done on a shoe-string and by the skin of our teeth but October 19th came and many people descended on the chosen camp site early one Saturday morning.

Before I continue, please do not take away with you the impression that I did all of the above heroically single-handed. I did not. David did as much as he could when time and emotion allowed. Lucy was an amazing help as was our core crew of Matt, Craig, Dodie, Nick and Sonia. Ah, Sonia. She who started out as a potential caterer and ended up being location manager and 2nd AD in some instances. She also had a small role to play in the film itself.

As did I. I failed to mention that. As well as attempting to learn the pre-production on the fly, I was also a co-director and one of the

Cadavers. Victor Cadaver, to be precise – named after my granddad – father to his zombie offspring and wife to Kelly, played by Vikki. In hindsight, I should have let something give. Being on set, chased for answers and dealing with problems as a producer is really difficult when I was also acting as a line producer (he or she who makes sure that people are where they are supposed to be at any given time). I was also trying to keep on top of continuity whilst making decisions as a co-director, sitting in make-up getting zombie-fied right before going on set to, um, "act".

I ain't Robert DeNiro. But I did an adequate job of playing, essentially, myself. But as a zombie.

It was truly exhausting. The weather was not our friend and the Indian Summer fucked off, within hours, morphing effortlessly into an Indian Monsoon. Comedy highlight of the day being a chap dressed as Alice In Wonderland chasing his tent across a field in the pissing rain. Alas, not for the film, just so he had somewhere to sleep that night.

Needless to say, nothing ran smoothly. Everything that could go wrong did go wrong. Luck was not on our side and the weather did not co-operate one bit. I was the first on set and the last off every day. In between, I had more pre-production, production and director duties to attend to before the next weekend's shooting. It was the most daunting thing I have ever done in my life: making a feature film. I threw myself in at the deep end and, with the aid of some arm bands – cunningly disguised as our awesome cast and crew – I just about managed to stay afloat. I was the proverbial swan, gracefully gliding above water whilst all hell is breaking loose underneath.

We wrapped on the 15th December after a final special effect, shot in my front garden. It was a very anti-climactic moment as I wasn't that involved in it. It was a small crew, no cast, so I became tea and mince pie boy. But that was OK. We had finished. Somehow, all those combined hours put in by a team of up to 30+ people, mounted to "Meet The Cadavers" being in the can.

CHAPTER XXVII:
MEANWHILE, BACK IN
THE REAL WORLD

Filming "Meet The Cadavers" at any time of year would have been hard work. Filming it during the busiest time of our year, every year, was idiotic.

Late October, we sell our SMELLYOURMUM.COM clobber at ComicCon in London. An event that now caters for over 100,000 people. It happens twice a year and is a big pay day for us and, without it, we wouldn't have been able to pay all those mounting Cadaver bills. It is a three day event but, of course, more than that is the preparation. For me, that doesn't amount to too much but for Vikki... well, that is 600 odd t-shirts she has to print by hand. Hard enough ordinarily; tricky as fuck when she is co-producing and co-starring in a film.

November and December are also our busiest months online with our tees. They make ideal presents and we sell hundreds, maybe thousands, during that time. All printed by Vikki and, unlike Expo, I do have to work my butt off during this period as well, sorting out all the orders, dealing with customers and getting the postage labels made up. Not as hard work as Vikki, but very, very time consuming.

The other massive hurdle was a festival we were booked to play at: Hard Rock Hell. This would be our third time playing, our first in the new location and the first with Rob. We were looking forward to it and, I must admit, even I was quite excited.

I did see it almost as a make-or-break gig though. Yes, I was quite excited by it, but not like I normally would be. I figured that one of two things would happen. Either, a) I would do the gig, think "what the fuck have I been missing?!" and it would re-ignite my passion for music or, b) I would come away with more questions than answers.

Driving to north Wales was long. We had to rehearse beforehand. Ordinarily, for something of this magnitude, we would rehearse the shit out of our set but, meh, I COULDN'T BE ARSED and was so busy with Cadavers, we just ran through it a couple of times. It was OK. We kind of remembered what to do.

Once we got to Wales, I got into the whole rock star thing. Walking around, having people come up to me, wanting photos, autographs and all that good shit. Me and Vikki took our new puppy, Skully, along for the ride. That is a dog that has lived a lot in a short time! Abandoned and picked up in Ireland, condemned to death but rescued to a centre in the south east. We got her in September and she came out on recces with us and even on to the film set. Her coming to be a rock n' roll dog seemed like the logical next step.

Certainly, she went down a treat in interviews. I had lined up about 10 or 11, solely to talk about "Meet The Cadavers". Most were obliging and I got a lot of press out of that weekend – I guess they were fed up with the usual rock and metal chat so, nattering to us about films and playing with our puppy made a nice break!

Before we were due to play, I plastered the venue with posters. Not band ones, but movie ones. I wanted everyone to come away from that event knowing about the film. I did a good job, everyone was talking about it that weekend.

However, we were there to do a job. The job of rock. We bundled into the bus to drive to the part of the venue where we would be playing. As is always the case when we play HRH, our time was shifted from a pretty good one to a very shit one, this time against the headliners Airbourne. I am not sure if this happened because "if anyone can compete, it is SLT" or just that we wouldn't complain too much.

There was a band unloading their gear when we arrived. They looked awesome – like a nuclear Twisted Sister. From Sweden, they completely had the look and I remember, again, having that uncomfortable feeling of being reminded that we no longer put in any effort. At the first Hard Rock Hell we did. That was us: all fake fire and lights and skulls and madness. It served us well. We got great press and a lot of attention. But, tonight, we were just jeans and T-shirts, plug in and play. Oh how the mighty had fallen.

I suspected nerves. I didn't really get any. I suspected adrenaline. I didn't really get any. I warmed up my voice a little – after all, it was a short set with no gig to follow the next day – and warmed up my body a lot. My knee was still a sore point.

We hit the stage and, yes, there was a good crowd. Extra good when you consider that the headline band was playing in another hall. And, for an unrehearsed bunch of people, we didn't play a bad set. I hit the right notes, made the right moves, got my abs out, got in the face of the people down the front. But, all the while, in the back of my mind, I was distracted, knowing that I was just going through the motions. No longer a jack rabbit of spontaneity, I was doing the minimum expected of me.

Before doing the show, I would have imagined coming off the stage in a ball of sweat and excitement; full of piss and vinegar and rock star swagger. The reality was, I came off, packed the stuff away, drove back to the chalet and had a hot chocolate, before heading back to the venue to see if anyone wanted to say anything nice.

A far cry from the first time we played when a queue of punters were lined up for us to sign CDs.

WE HIT THE STAGE AND, YES, THERE WAS A GOOD CROWD. EXTRA GOOD WHEN YOU CONSIDER THAT THE HEADLINE BAND WAS PLAYING IN ANOTHER HALL. AND, FOR AN UNREHEARSED BUNCH OF PEOPLE, WE DIDN'T PLAY A BAD SET."

To be fair, nice things say, they did. For some, it was the best gig of the weekend. We got that a lot. And it meant a lot to me but it added to the fraudulent feeling. I would have been happier if people said "what happened, you used to be so good?", because that is how I felt on the inside. I smiled through it though, took the photos and signed the CDs all with good grace. I genuinely am pleased that people enjoyed us – my bad feeling and discomfort comes from knowing that I did not put my best foot forward.

When the weekend was done, I was glad to get out of there. It had been the first time we had seen our guitar player, Rob, in several months. It is July 2016 as I finish the final edit of this book and, although we haven't *officially* split up or disbanded, December 2013 was actually the last time I saw him.

I did not know that would be the case back in 2013, as I did not know what fate had in store for Vikki and I in 2014.

CHAPTER XXVIII:
2014, PART ONE

B arely into a brand new year and the edit for "Meet The Cadavers" started. Vikki and I had booked ourselves a flight and accommodation to Cannes for the film festival taking place that May. The ideal situation would have been to have taken along with us a trailer and rough cut of the film. It would be tight but if me, David and Matt (camera operator but also assistant editor) pulled out all the stops, we could do it.

A good job was done, initially, and we raced through the first eight scenes with a further four very roughly pieced together. You know what, we might be able to do this. Then Matt had to quit.

Not his fault. He wasn't being paid to edit, doing it out of love of the project and a friendship that had grown during the making of. So, when a dream job came up for him to be a camera operator for Tottenham Hotspur, he jumped at it. I think he thought he could carry on with the edit but, the truth of the matter was that, with the best intentions in the world, he just did not have the time.

Bollocks. This was a major hurdle as David was already editing a film now two years in the making, his "Blaze Of Gory" anthology. Yes, he could still edit Cadavers, but it would be a very slow process. So things ground to a halt and I tried to work out what to do next.

Before I had a chance to come to any conclusions, David offered me the opportunity to direct one of the segments for Blaze Of Gory, "Spawn Of The Devil". How could I say No? I didn't want to say no, for a start, and what an amazing opportunity to put into practise everything I had learned on Cadavers.

Almost as soon as I agreed, the hard work started. He sent over the script as it stood and I added a further 12 pages, expanding the story, defining the characters further and adding some other elements that I felt made the work stronger. David was more than happy with this and he was even happier when we cast ██████████ (██████████ founder, ████████ daughter) in the lead role.

Pre-production was much easier this time around. For a start, I had a much better idea of what I was doing and, not being in the film meant that I could concentrate solely on my one job, that of director. We pulled together most of the Cadaver Crew to help out and also cast some familiar faces. I was really enjoying this collaborative family that we had and I loved the idea of making more and more films with them.

Filming took place one weekend early March. It was cold, but the weather stayed dry. ████████ was a complete trooper, having all sorts of disgusting things happen to her without complaint. She suffered more than any of us, covered in gore and ooze, having to lay around on cold floors. Lucy also pulled out a trump card with some of the special effects she put together. This was turning out to be a nice little production.

Prior to filming, David and I had worked out a pretty comprehensive shot list – complete with story board – something we neglected to do on Cadavers. This made things much easier as everyone knew what the hell was going on. They say that the best way to learn something is to just attempt it, and it is very true. You can read all the books in the world (as I think I did) but it is not until you get your hands dirty that you REALLY know the score.

I hold my own as a director. Being a band leader for so long, and a performer, I am confident which, in turn, instils confidence in others. You need that. The cast and crew have to be able to place their complete trust in you, knowing that you have half a clue. Of course, I do not know much of the technical side of things (although I am slowly learning) but I know the feel that I am after and the kind of shots I like, along with the performances I want. I will never be a director that holds the camera himself (I don't think); I will be the kind that paints the canvas while others hold the brushes.

2014 was shaping up to be a very exciting year!

NB: *Just prior to the publication of this book, I learnt that the segment I directed would not be released as shot due to an injunction filed against the producers by one of the principals. Rather than go through a protracted legal case which they can ill afford, the decision has been made to push ahead with the release, with scenes from my film inserted into some of the remaining nine. I don't know what could be so objectionable about being shagged by a guy dressed as the devil in a cow shed to make them want to pull out but, there you have it. That's showbiz!*

I HOLD MY OWN AS A DIRECTOR. BEING A BAND LEADER FOR SO LONG, AND A PERFORMER, I AM CONFIDENT WHICH, IN TURN, INSTILS CONFIDENCE IN OTHERS. YOU NEED THAT. THE CAST AND CREW HAVE TO BE ABLE TO PLACE THEIR COMPLETE TRUST IN YOU, KNOWING THAT YOU HAVE HALF A CLUE."

CHAPTER XXIX:
2014, PART TWO

My nan died later that same month. It was not totally unexpected. In fact, I had predicted it in my diary at the end of 2013. Not through any kind of insane insight, but because she was a 94 year old woman who had suffered with Alzheimer's for at least ten years and was in failing health.

I remember walking around East Grinstead the day it happened. Vikki had had an operation on her eye in February and we were in town for a check up. I had heard from mum who'd said a couple of things that made it pretty clear the end was imminent. I said to Vikki "I think that nan will die today".

The call came about 10.30pm. I didn't answer it. I couldn't face it, even though I knew what it was. Of course, I had to call back, I just needed that moment to compose myself. As anyone that has watched the living nightmare that is Alzheimer's will know, witnessing a loved one disappear into themselves is a very cruel trick. This lady that showed me such love – this lady who worshipped the ground I walk on – no longer knew my name. She hadn't done for years. She didn't know her own name. She required 24/7 care and was as helpless as a new born.

I'd been grieving for nan for at least seven years. These people we love are slowly taken away from us, day by day. When she first started regressing, she would have moments of clarity and I could tease her forgetfulness. But it soon went altogether. For a while, she would call me George (my Granddad), which I did kind of like, but it wouldn't be long before she had no speech and the light in her eyes had gone out. Physically, she was in situ but her mind was gone for ever.

So when the end came, I was not expecting much sadness, I was expecting relief. And I *was* relieved, but I was also incredibly sad. Maybe there was a little voice in the back of my head that believed there was a chance she could come back, one last time, to recognise us all. Her death was the finality that confirmed what we already knew: she was lost to us for ever.

And, with that day came the loss of my childhood. Maybe that is an odd thing to say as I was 41 at the time, but I always connected my nan and granddad at Bookham with my childhood. Bookham had been the house I practically grew up in, the house I felt most comfortable in, the house that entertained all my favourite people in the world every Christmas. The house whose lights finally were switched off to us all, one last time.

The next day we met at my brother's house as it was Mother's Day weekend. This pre-arranged date still happened, which was lovely, and I think it helped us all being with each other that day. There was a lot of laughter and reminiscing with very few tears. It was quite joyous and I felt much better after it.

Of course, what follows next is all the shitty stuff. House clearing and funerals. I wanted to help with the house clearing – it felt like my final chance to connect with these people that were my life, and the last thing that I could do for them. It was a mixed bag of emotions. On the one hand, it was beautiful to relive so many happy memories that would be ignited by a smell, or an ornament. On the other, there was such sadness to know that this whole part of my life was forever now behind a closed door.

Vikki and I had quite a lot of my grandparent's furniture. We didn't have much of a purpose for it, initially, as our house was very small, but it needed saving. I must admit, now, I love walking around and seeing these reminders. Every day I get to be with my nan and granddad and feel a part of them with me. In a way, I have created a Petit Bookham – they would have loved that.

Things slowly settled down and we got into a routine. We would visit Bookham and help clear stuff at the weekends, deal with business and film stuff during the week, all the while preparing to go to Cannes in May, shortly followed by the London Expo upon our return.

Cannes was very exciting. We only had four days out there, but we got lucky as a transport strike meant that we were able to have impromptu meetings with various executives. I know we made some good contacts and it was nice being out on the Riviera, soaking up the sun and feeling slightly awkward at the ostentatious displays of wealth around. Still, it opened our eyes to a whole other world, a world that we were trying to make footprints in. We couldn't wait to get home to start hitting those business cards!

Of course, we had to get Expo out of the way first. It is always a "get it out of the way" kind of weekend. The enjoyment has waned and it is just an exercise in turnover. Vikki was slightly off her game as, when she had called her Granddad upon our return from Cannes, he hadn't sounded so good. By the time of Expo, he'd gone into hospital to have a few tests. Once the weekend was over, we would go and visit him.

Vikki's mum, Julie, had warned us that Pete, Vikki's Granddad, wasn't in a good way. But she had said this before and I didn't pay it much mind. So when we visited Granddad Pete to find him on an oxygen machine looking half the man we were used to seeing, it was a shock. We all put on a brave face – as did he – and Vikki showed him the photos from Cannes, knowing how much of a kick he would get out of that. He was clearly very tired, so we stayed for only an hour before heading back.

As is often the case in times of crisis, the law of Sod kicks in just to make things harder than they need to be. A failing alternator was putting a spanner in our works and we had to try and squeeze in the time to get that sorted. As I type, I know two things are fact: 1) we visited Pete two days consecutively and, 2) at some point, we got the alternator fixed. How that happened though, I don't know. You just go on autopilot.

I think we were actually going to leave a day between visits, but Vikki woke me early the next morning crying. My first thought was that he had gone in the night but it wasn't that. In some ways, it was worse. Julie had called to say that it would be any moment, so the race to Hastings began.

Journeys like that are the worst. Not knowing if you will make it on time, not knowing what state your loved-one might be in. On this day, Granddad Pete was clearly in much more distress than the day before. He was a large man, statuesque with giant hands and a cheeky face. He was still all that on this day and stoic in the face of death.

He knew his time was up. We knew his time was up. He showed a bravery that I cannot comprehend, holding himself to the best of his abilities so as not to overly concern his loved ones. He cracked jokes, flirted with the nurse and only got serious when the palliative care nurse arrived and he asked for a private chat.

We all knew what he was asking her. A Do Not Resuscitate had already been ordered and his wishes would have been for the swiftest exit he could have. And who could blame him. He knew he didn't need to hang on for the family's sake. His only regret was that he would never get to meet his great grandson, who was born just a couple of weeks later.

I gave him a kiss on his head when we left, something I had never done before. I held his hand, said Goodbye and, as I left he broke me with these words: "I wish you every success as a director". I barely made it out of his sight before bursting into tears. Of course, this was not a moment about me as around me were a granddaughter, a grandson and a daughter who were all suffering way more than I. So I composed myself the best I could and tried to be there for each of them.

Granddad Pete died later that night.

CHAPTER XXX:
2014, PART THREE

Had rather a low key Birthday that June. Neither of us were particularly in the mood to celebrate; we had a funeral looming and were still clearing out my nan's place.

So, when our landlady of 11 years let us know that she was putting her main house on the market with the intention of moving into the house we lived in, it was another blow. Another shock to our already depleted systems.

Although no eviction notice was given, we had a choice to make. Our landlady's house was expensive – chances are it wasn't going to sell quickly - but we really did not want that looming over our heads. After all, if left with a month to get the kind of place we liked, we'd be unlikely to find it.

Immediately, we started to look for new digs. We have a particular love of pretty, rural locations, old buildings with no neighbours. Add this to the mix of being self-employed with pets, the search ahead seemed pretty daunting.

It wasn't long before we realised that there was very little chance of finding the kind of place that we liked in the kind of location that we liked in the south east of England. Quite by chance, we found a massive house in Scotland from the 1930s. Deco in appearance, we couldn't believe that this mini-mansion was half the rent that we were currently paying. A quick Google revealed that this was no fluke: Scotland was fucking cheap.

My nan on my dad's side was Scottish. It took me quite a while to understand her accent (remember, I didn't meet her until mum met dad, when I was six) but I got it in the end. She was such a kind, lovely lady. I never heard a cross word from her. She was always laughing and smiling, filling my face with sweets and apple pies. I stayed at their house aged 15 when my parents went on holiday. She made the best sausage and chips: I would have gladly killed for her chip butties.

Naturally, this laid a latent fondness for Scotland that surged forth when the notion of moving there was first mooted. This was now our goal: we were to move to Scotland!

It wasn't long before we found some incredible places for rent and contacted the agent. In fact, it was at Granddad Pete's wake where we first saw a serious contender, The Owl House. A large building set in 60 acres of forest in a dark sky area of Ayrshire. To take her mind off the events of the day, Vikki gave the agent a call and we were invited to submit an application.

Here was when we discovered the rather annoying nature of the Scottish rental system. Unlike in England, when you apply to rent a property in Scotland, you are submitted to the potential landlord, along with every other bugger who has applied. Naturally, a couple of self employed people that look funny and, when Googled, turn up all kinds of outrageousness, are not usually top of the Yes list.

We put our best foot forward, however, and attempted to ingratiate ourselves to the agent in the hope she might put in a good word for us. We promised all kinds of guarantees and even offered to pay a few months' rent up front. Annoyingly, it wasn't until we drove up to Scotland to view the place that we were told it would only be available for a maximum of two years. We were looking for longer term so, when our application was rejected, we weren't too bothered.

The other serious contender was a Victorian manor house called Dahlwat Farm. We flew up to visit it, unsupervised, and had a good look around. It was quite dilapidated but it was absolutely massive. We could literally lose each other in it. The size concerned me from a heating point of view but, from a space point of view, I loved it. I loved the idea of us being Lord & Lady of the manor so, when we made a second visit after some decorating had been done we were, for the second time, sold.

Again, we went through the process of application. I spent hours writing a letter to the landlord, to introduce myself and to tell them what an honour it would be to live in a house like that. I wasn't blowing fluff up their trouser leg - I love old houses and the opportunity to become part of their DNA excites me, thoroughly.

Again, we were rejected. No reason given. This was a frustrating situation; an annoying procedure and a bloody expensive one. We were some 450 miles away so every trip cost a lot of money; money we could not afford to keep spending only to get rejected.

For a couple of months, we had the same daily procedure, the same drudge. It went like this: get up, check emails for new listings. Look at new listings. Rule out the absolute No's. Make a Maybe pile and make contact with the Yes'. We would then scour the various websites that list property for a few hours, constantly hitting "Refresh" on the email to receive the latest listings there. It was a boring, tiresome, seemingly endless process.

All the while, we had a deadline in our head. We needed to be moved by September as, from that month until the end of the year, we would be way too busy to contemplate moving. What made this so stressful was that it was a situation that was out of our hands. Any day, our landlady could have given us a move date. If that had fallen in, say, November, we would have been well and truly fucked.

Necessity is the mother of invention and it was this kind of pressure that made me suggest to Vikki that we actually advertised ourselves. I was quite surprised when she agreed, but agree she did, so we put an advert on Gumtree: "Self-employed couple with a dog and two cats seek remote/rural detached property with ground, preferably with garage."

I think it was the next day that we got the first response. I was surprised. The property was unsuitable (the amount of people that think a slightly big garden and a terraced house qualifies as rural is frightening) but several others got in touch.

Then one night, whilst doing my cardio, Vikki received an email from a "Jez & Margie". It was a friendly email, containing a link to their property on an estate agent's website. I was having one of my less positive moments so, when Vikki said "this will be the one, it'll be perfect", I scoffed at her. She then started making "wow" sounds and I thought she was taking the piss. She showed me the picture.

It looked perfect. Just the kind of house we would dream of living in. Scrap that, I didn't even know that you COULD live in a house like this. It was a 17th Century Bastle house, high up in the Northern Pennines near the old England/Scotland border. Many original features were preserved and it seemed to have plenty of room. There also seemed to be a pretty decent view. But there was a catch: it was up for sale, not rent.

We had to get to the bottom of this, so Vikki rang the number in the email and found out what the situation was. After a couple of bad rental experiences, the owners had reluctantly decided to sell as they were fed up dealing with bad tenants. However, they hadn't had any bites in the few years it had been up for sale and they had, just that night, decided that they would rent it out again; they loved the area and did not want to move. It was then they looked on Gumtree and saw our advert.

Fate is a funny thing. Some people call it luck, but I don't subscribe to that. Vikki and I made as many opportunities as we could to find a place. The fact that our paths crossed with the paths of Jez & Margie was a coincidence. A wonderful coincidence, yes, but we worked hard at helping that take place. "Luck" is simply preparation meeting opportunity.

There was a scary couple of days as we had to wait for one final house viewing to take place. That was it, I was convinced that we would lose out again. I try to be positive but, when faced with situations like this, I prepare myself for bad news as I would rather be wrong and delighted than wrong and devastated.

I was wrong. And I was delighted! We on a plane later that week flying to Newcastle airport. We then hired a car, driving the near 50 miles to a small parish called Kirkhaugh, right on the Cumbria / Northumberland border. Jez and Margie were there to greet us and showed us around. There are three things I will always remember about the house on that first visit: 1) the smell in the room we now call the Vault Room. It smelt like a castle. An old wood fire's long-burned embers permeating the fabric of that space. 2) The stairs. They were made of bonkers. Hundreds of years of footsteps had worn the solid stone to make them concave. Magic. And, finally, 3) The views. The views. THE VIEWS. They were epic and vast and took my breath away.

Then came The Chat. We had flown up there unaware of what the actual rent was. Not only that, but just because we wanted the place didn't mean we would get it. After all, to a lot of people, we are an unsavoury pair. Especially if you Google us.

Jez & Margie Googled us. Thank fuck they are considerably more liberal and fun loving than most as they had no problem with us, what we did or how we earned our filthy lucre. We spoke for a couple of hours and then the slightly awkward moment came, a moment that had remained unspoken. In a strange way, we had been trying to sell ourselves to them whilst they had been trying to sell themselves to us. As it happens, neither of us needed a sales pitch as it was a natural fit. We wanted in and they wanted us in. A couple of formalities later, High Row was ours for the foreseeable future.

Of course, there was a downside. Well, two, really. The first being that we would be a long way from our families. Both our families live in the south east of England and we were moving as far away from them as we possibly could whilst remaining in the country. This did not go unnoticed! The second downside was the lack of garage. We had that classic Porsche 928 from 1989 and I really wanted to be able to protect it from the elements, as it was my understanding that there would be many more of those to contend with in the north.

We were advised to get a 4x4. I had no previous desire to own a 4x4 and, as a result, knew fuck all about them. Vikki and I exchanged an endless search for houses for an endless search for a 4x4. It didn't help that, every time I settled on a model to look for, a quick bit of research would reveal a cataclysmic list of common faults all of nightmare proportions. Once I drove a Range Rover though, I wanted one of those. I was surprised at the luxurious interior and the drive itself. It reminded me a lot of my Granddad's old Mercedes.

After a few weeks' search, I spotted one in Brighton that I really liked the look of. It was a bit more money than we wanted to spend, but it was a good looking motor and was the slightly later model that avoided a lot of the common problems inherent with earlier Range Rovers. We went for a test drive, struck a deal and took delivery of a 2001 4.6 V8 Vogue in Monte Carlo Blue.

The end was in sight. Apart from the logistics of getting us and our stuff the 300 miles from our old house to the new, we had somehow managed to find a place and agree a date to move in: 10th September.

CHAPTER XXXI:
2014, PART FOUR

The night before we were due to leave, our old landlady, Diane and her husband, Alan, invited us over to their house to say Goodbye. It was a lovely gesture and, although we had a big day ahead, we, of course, accepted the invitation.

We arrived to find that they had also invited some of the neighbours and friends that we had made during our 11 years in Burstow. And so followed a really nice evening in the company of people whom we would never had encountered had we not accidentally moved into their neighbourhood. I am sure they feared the worst when this funny looking couple with an old black hearse bundled themselves into the quaint cottage, but they never had cause to complain. That evening was spent reminiscing, sharing stories, sharing photographs of our soon-to-be new locale and saying Goodbye. It was really nice.

Time moves on and the next day was as stressful as most moving days are. Considering that we were moving so far away, we handled the problems well. After all, people being late and stuck in traffic isn't the end of the world, it's just bloody inconvenient. Of course, our military style planning went completely out of the window and every mover arrived at once. Suddenly we had to deal with two large moving vans and the transporter for the 928, as they all descended upon us.

The car went off without a hitch but it soon became evident that we had way more stuff than the movers expected. We had to leave quite a lot behind in the garage and arrange, at a later date, for another mover to bring it up. Annoying and expensive but, what are you gonna do?

Soon it was time for us to say goodbye to our home of 11 years. Vikki and I had spent most of our relationship in that house, building some kind of future for ourselves, building a band, building a brand and going through all the life-cycles that occur over a long period of time: births, marriages, deaths. Good times, bad times. A long time. It was strange seeing the place empty, void of what made it our home. Suddenly it was the same blank box it was prior to us moving in.

After a farewell at my mum and dad's and my last chance to grab a Chinese takeaway (a rare treat since made extinct due to location and new dietary restrictions), a quick detour back to Burstow to collect the animals and, that was it; it was midnight and we were on our way to a new life.

We drove through the night, excited and nervous. I was most worried about our stuff arriving in one piece and, let's not beat around the bush, moving into a new place and having to find homes for everything is a tiresome chore. After just over eight hours, we arrived, greeted by our new landlord and landlady, Jez and Margie. We stuck the animals somewhere safe and then the movers arrived.

I made the mistake of carrying a box or two in. It wasn't long before I became one of the movers by default. So, despite being shattered after a long drive without sleep, I spent the next few hours moving heavy boxes into various rooms. I didn't realise how tired I was until later that evening, when we had to drive to Hexham (approximately 25 miles away) to the nearest DIY store to get some pipe for the washing machine. I found myself almost asleep at the wheel and I had to pull over just to nap for 20 minutes or so. In all our years of touring, I have NEVER had to do that before, so I must have been shattered.

The next few weeks were spent settling ourselves in, dressing the house with our furniture and taking hundreds of fucking photographs. I apologise now to anyone that followed me on Facebook or Twitter at that time as I know my feeds have just been full of these.

Barely had the dust settled, we found ourselves heading back down south for our niece's naming ceremony. We were away a few days, taking the opportunity to visit Vikki's mum as well but we hated being away. Obviously, it was lovely seeing everyone and we wanted to be around them, but we missed High Row dreadfully. This scenario has repeated many times since and, each time, we cannot wait to get home.

We were – are – gloriously happy in Kirkhaugh, Northumberland. Every day I wake, opening the curtains excited as to what the view will be that day. Will the mountains opposite be backlit by glorious blue skies, or will I not be able to see them due to low flying clouds? We can experience every season in the space of an hour up here; it is crazy and exhilarating.

After the madness of moving, we had the madness of Christmas. Not just the 12 days of, but the preceding months as well, due to our busy online shop. I am not complaining – money is always welcome – but it did mean that we hadn't had a chance to truly relax into our new house and environment. In fact, it wasn't until after the very last trip down south, early in 2015, that we finally had those moments. It was bliss.

CHΛPTER XXXII:
2015-2016 SO, NOW WHΛT?

T hat, right there, is the big question I have been trying to answer; it is the reason that I wrote this book in the first place. I had hoped that this little bit of analysis would help me clear the brain path to what lay ahead. It didn't.

I wrote those words a year ago. I finished the book on a downer, with no conclusion. It sat doing nothing as I continued on my journey. Today, I decided to edit this book to prepare it for publication. You see, I now have some answers.

My life used to be easy. I knew exactly what I wanted to do from quite an early age and went about pursuing that. I managed to achieve a lot of what I dreamt of musically but then simply stopped enjoying it. I didn't want many toys as long as I had an old Porsche to drive. When we moved, I sold the car. A small price I am willing to pay for living here, but I never thought I would see that day either.

Everything I thought I knew I was, wiped out and challenged in a matter of months. In fact, it lead to a total loss of identity and, for a short period, I didn't care about what I wore or how I appeared to the outside world. For the first time in my life, I did not want to stick out like a sore thumb as I needed to work out who the hell I was. For a long while, this left me extremely confused.

I no longer was this one thing I was certain I was.

But, why limit myself to being just one thing?[1] I enjoy lots of different activities and, if I can make money doing any or all of them, that's even better. I am part artist, part business man, part guru. (Mostly dickhead.)

It has taken me the best part of the two years we have lived up here for me to finally have the vague outline of A Plan. How did I come to that? Well, I asked myself one question, *"If I won the lottery, what would I do?"*. I am not one for sitting around on my arse and I came up with the following:

1) I would write
2) I would make films
3) I would travel
4) I would buy and sell art and antiquities
5) I would purchase an old farm house in rural Italy to renovate
Let's run through that list.

I have always written. Be it a song, screenplay or book, it is words from my head onto paper. Or onto T-Shirts. My particular writing interests lay in both comedic and motivational/help yourself (my preferred term for self help). I love making people laugh; I enjoy the challenge of a perfectly formed joke. I also love exploring the human psyche and trying to help others come to terms with their own. The other books being written fall into both those categories.

Films....ARGH! Don't mention "Meet The Cadavers"! I won't bore you with the details, but it has become an editing nightmare. For some reason, finding someone to do it hasn't worked out. Maybe it is too personal a film for me and I can only see it one way. Who knows? However, this problem (remember, a problem is an opportunity in disguise!) did force me to get an editing programme to learn how to edit in case I ended up doing it. To learn to edit, I needed to make little films, which forced me into launching ZVTV, our YouTube Entertainment Channel (www.zvtv.co.uk). In turn, this has made me appreciate how much I absolutely LOVE making little YouTube videos. It has also made me realise how much I LOATHE editing! Regardless,

"Meet The Cadavers" WILL get finished. I will continue to make ZVTV clips and I will make other films.

Travelling has ceased temporarily since moving. Many factors in this, none of them very interesting. I guess other things are a priority at the moment. However, several of the projects I am working on can eventually lead to travel so, for the moment, I am content staying put.

Since moving, I have started buying and selling antiquities, vintage items and collectables. However, my tastes and desires are way beyond where I am at the moment. I want to get away from the smaller items and more toward larger items of great beauty. I am getting more confident and have recently put my money where my mouth is, investing in some contemporary artists. The wonderful thing about dealing in such items is being the custodian of them. I love looking at beautiful objects so surrounding myself with them is a joy. Alas, that world can be a stuffy one, which tends to get on my tits.

Another reason for the art investment (alongside other, more traditional ones) is to roll the dice that can eventually achieve that last goal: to buy a farmhouse in Italy and renovate it. Make no bones about it, by dedicating my life up until this point to rock, I gave up my chance of buying a house or building a career that I could retire early from. It is not a decision I regret in the slightest but, to have that Italian adventure, I need to have more do$h than I have now.

Rather accidentally, I started trading and investing in stocks and shares. Seeing an opportunity when the market collapsed post-Brexit, I bought some shares in banks and construction companies. They had fallen way below their true value so, once they corrected themselves, I had done quite well. This got me hooked on the whole process and I now find myself back at self-imposed school, trying to learn and

SINCE MOVING, I HAVE STARTED BUYING AND SELLING ANTIQUITIES, VINTAGE ITEMS AND COLLECTABLES. HOWEVER, MY TASTES AND DESIRES ARE WAY BEYOND WHERE I AM AT THE MOMENT."

educate myself about something I never expected to have anything to do with. I find it oddly exciting, turning air into more expensive air. Or, at least, that's how this magic voodoo stock market shit appears to me!

Finally, music. Where am I with that? After all, there is a good chance that you may only be reading this because you know me through my band. Well, SPiT LiKE THiS is currently on permanent vacation and will remain so for the foreseeable future. At the moment, at least, I don't miss it.

[1] Since writing this, I have discovered a term for my seeming lack of direction or, as I now like to think of it, broad range of interests. I appear to be a Multipotentialite: *"a person who has many different interests and creative pursuits in life." [puttylike.com]*. We are taught from birth the notion of finding our "one true calling" which, when I lost mine, caused great anxiety. But, you know what? I don't think I have one true calling, I have many and I intend to explore them all!

EPILOGUE:
I DID IT MY WAY

Some people call it stubbornness. Others a need to be right. Is it ego or is it artistic foresight? Whatever it is or isn't, I have it: the My Way Or The Highway gene.

I have thought long and hard about this trait of mine. After all, on so many occasions, I have taken suggestions and advice from people that are far more learned than I and completely ignored them. Or, decided to "go another way". For me, it is not ego. It is not that I think I know best. It's not even that I think I am right. I am simply following a gut instinct to do things in a particular fashion.

It is the artist in me. For better or worse, right or wrong, if I don't follow my instinctive urge, I will always be left feeling flat. I should mention, this has lead to very little success, so I cannot justify my actions by pointing toward a huge pile of cash and yelling "SHUT UP" to those that dare question me. But it has lead to a modicum of artistic achievement of which I am proud. A small catalogue that I readily put my name to.

Compromise is a word I am beginning to learn. Sometimes, there is no option than to compromise if you want to move forward with a project. I prefer to think of compromise more along the lines of adapting to circumstance. I will only compromise in areas I am happy to, however, and never will I compromise my moral code.

We are only here once and have just one opportunity to leave any kind of mark. Whether I remain on the fringes of success or have a certified smash remains to be seen. If, one day, something I produce connects with a large audience, that will be amazing. It will make up for all the times I doubted myself but went with my gut anyway. It will prove me right.

However, if that day never comes and I am destined to produce works that bring joy and entertainment to a small group of enthusiasts, that still makes me one hell of a happy bugger, because who doesn't want to enrich lives, if only a few?

I believe this is a trait that has served me well and one that I will continue with until I am no more. I've always been a General, never a soldier, and whilst I recognise that it tends to be the soldiers that do all the hard graft, you need a good General to point them in the right direction. I have been fortunate in that I have always found my little armies easily.

If you believe in what you do, others will believe in you. That is why you must follow your own truth. People will always spot a liar. It may make you unpopular to some and it will lead to many, awkward, unwelcome stand-offs, but life is full of those anyway, so you may as well get what you want out of them.

When I wrote this, I was at a crossroads in my life and I genuinely didn't know which way to turn. There would be no right or wrong answer, but the choices were mine to make. Granted, some may be disappointed with some of the decisions, but disappointment is part of life. However much I loved having people enjoy my band's music – and still do - I only ever made it for me and performed it for myself. My heart is no longer in it and it would be fraudulent of me to stand on a stage and take people's money now it has ceased to be a burning passion.

Most people stumble into a job after they leave school and stay with it until they retire, or until it is too late to do what they really want. It took me a long time to admit to myself that being in a band was over for me and it took me a longer time to work out my next manoeuvre. I have many sides to my personality and my interests reflect that. I don't like to be pigeon-holed or to be predictable. Expect the unexpected, as they say.

As long as I remain entertaining and entertained, I will be doing alright.

A series of unfortunate events bought us to this place at this time in our lives. I don't know what would have happened if my nan or Vikki's granddad hadn't passed and I find myself feeling guilt whenever I dwell on the fact that my current situation – a situation I am happy within - is brought about by the deaths of loved-ones. How do you marry up these conflicting scenarios? I've still not worked that out.

Vikki bought me a coaster one Christmas. On it is printed, "Do more of what makes you happy". This is very sound advice and I tried to take note of the moments I was at my happiest to help formulate my future plans.

Do your current plans make you happy? If not, what the fuck are you going to do about it?

Zion
Northumberland
December 2016

IF YOU BELIEVE IN WHAT YOU DO, OTHERS WILL BELIEVE IN YOU. THAT IS WHY YOU MUST FOLLOW YOUR OWN TRUTH. PEOPLE WILL ALWAYS SPOT A LIAR. IT MAY MAKE YOU UNPOPULAR TO SOME AND IT WILL LEAD TO MANY, AWKWARD, UNWELCOME STAND-OFFS, BUT LIFE IS FULL OF THOSE ANYWAY, SO YOU MAY AS WELL GET WHAT YOU WANT OUT OF THEM."

Printed in Great Britain
by Amazon